GRACIOUSLY ASSERTIVE

GRACIOUSLY ASSERTIVE

How Becoming A BETTER HUMAN BEING Makes You A BETTER LEADER

YASMIN DAVIDDS, PsyD

morehouse PUBLISHING

Morehouse Publishing
19 East 34th Street
New York, NY 10016

Morehouse Publishing is an imprint of Church Publishing Incorporated.

Cover design by David Rotstein
Typeset by Nord Compo

A record of this book is available from the Library of Congress.

ISBN 978-1-64065-699-4 (hardcover)
ISBN 978-1-64065-700-7 (ebook)

This book is dedicated to my family.

First, to my daughter, Divina, who has been my inspiration since the day she was born. Thank you for giving me the gift of being your mother.

To my love, Luis Arandia, for loving me and always doing everything in your power to take good care of me. I love you. And to Carol Hasegawa, for raising such an amazing son.

To my Mami for loving me unconditionally and fostering my purpose in life.

To the leadership team of the Dr. Yasmin Davidds Leadership Institute, for your continuous commitment and dedication to our cause of empowering women leaders.

And . . .

To the inspiring alumni of my leadership programs who have courageously shared their stories in this book. Thank you for the honor of letting me include them. They will inspire people everywhere.

CONTENTS

FOREWORD

For many of us, there's a universal and unique longing to improve . . . to foster stronger relationships, achieve greater successes, and experience personal growth. While the concept seems straightforward, navigating the path to becoming a better version of ourselves often requires a guiding hand.

Graciously Assertive: How Becoming a Better Human Being Makes You a Better Leader is a road map, offering the best routes to becoming better humans and better leaders, while sharing continued guidance for improving your life and career overall.

As infants, we struggle to get on all fours, crawl, and then transform from a wobbly toddler into a marathon-running youngster. Our success in walking is achieved by instinct, desire, and need. Instinct told us it was achievable. Desire and need propelled us to accomplish it.

As adult human beings, instinct, need, and desire are not enough to achieve the goal of becoming the best person, best parent, best partner, or the best leader. Reaching the pinnacle of your best requires creating real transformation that is learned and earned. And, like a good education, this valuable transformation will not crumble and cannot be taken from you.

With *Graciously Assertive*, Dr. Yasmin Davidds offers a real and clear path to the reader's transformation to becoming the best human being possible. That might sound like hyperbole, but after reading and embracing the knowledge presented in this book, I know this to be true.

The cornerstones of this transformational guidebook are the 8 Pillars of Graciously Assertive Leadership. These guidelines to successful living provide a foundation for current and future leaders to become true, solid, and better at their tasks. These pillars are Self-Awareness, Social Awareness, Self-Regulation, Self-Compassion, Gratitude, Zero Tolerance for Judgment, Healthy Boundaries, and Graciously Assertive Communication.

Each pillar is equally needed and important, and together, they strengthen your growth and capacity to become the best version of yourself. At first glance, you may feel some of them don't fit your life or style. However, I urge you to give them a try. Embracing all eight may seem daunting, but once you see the positive changes and feel their transformative power, the results fold into an origami figurine, strengthening one's ability to do more and do better.

I'm a busy person. I felt there wasn't a time slot in my daily schedule to "become a better person," but I learned differently by reading this book, aptly titled *Graciously Assertive: How Becoming a Better Human Being Makes You a Better Leader*. I'm grateful Dr. Davidds utilized a style of writing that is deep, yet easy to comprehend. Her philosophy is intense, but presented in manageable statements that encourage the reader, saying "seek and you shall receive." There is no mystery about how to begin our quest to become the best person we can be, the person we want to be.

By offering this easy-to-use guide that points to deep and lasting shifts in our manner of living, *Graciously Assertive* is a double-edged sword of truth and possibility. This book, once read and absorbed, can create distinct and real shifts to our emotional and spiritual core, positively altering how we think, feel, and act toward our world, our community, and our soul. Also, it is a manual, not to change who you are, but to guide your transformation into the true loving and caring leader that you already are.

Reading this book, I understood transformation isn't an instant success. Instead, it is a series of tiny, almost indiscernible shifts in thinking and in doing. After each chapter, I felt and experienced transformations—some emotional, others practical.

One transformation was particularly simple, yet immensely powerful. I had been working twelve-hour days, seven days a week, almost every week. As an engaged member of an extended family and a public servant with over one million constituents, any available fifteen-minute slot of my seven-day work week is scheduled, leaving no time to envision what "better" looks like in any aspect of my life. I felt there just wasn't any time to think about becoming better, much less to experience a transformation.

Dr. Davidds' guide encouraged me to take what I thought was a deficiency (time) and turn it into a strength (use time well). The teachings in this book gifted me the right to take a few moments in my day to imagine how I could elevate the quality of leadership in my world, particularly with my staff. Those few moments made a huge difference in my performance as a leader.

The first pillar of *Graciously Assertive* is defined as Self-Awareness. At the heart of this pillar is comprehending one's strengths, weaknesses, triggers, and emotions. This enables leaders to anticipate their responses in specific situations and make deliberate choices for effective reactions.

Embracing self-awareness caused me to stop, reflect, and set time aside to understand my work process, my hierarchy of duties, commitments, and goals, and ask, "How's that working for me?" I discovered that to become a better leader, I needed to set an example for those around me.

Self-care? It was nonexistent in my life. Pillar 6 encourages setting healthy boundaries, and I knew in my heart the importance of taking a minute to reflect, a minute to breathe, a minute to just analyze my surroundings, but I didn't embrace it until I read this book. In doing so, I received two precious gifts. I'm transforming into a person who cares for herself, body and soul, and I am setting an example for my staff to do the same. Members of my staff have since become better rested and more confident individuals who are ready to conquer the world on a daily basis.

This book offered a clear path to changing my process in order to become an example to those around me, resulting in them becoming better people and better leaders themselves. It created a tsunami of transformation in my life.

And I didn't stop with that win. I explored how each of the 8 Pillars relates to every aspect of my job and my life. I asked myself another question: What is my role in the behaviors, patterns, and attitudes I choose for myself that have a direct impact on others?

In this guide, the notion of celebrating our daily victories and setbacks is explored while emphasizing how they are equally important in our growth toward becoming better and to our authentic transformation. There's nothing I enjoy more than celebrating a victory, but I don't have the tools to celebrate a setback. Most of us don't do setbacks well. Often our standards are set high, and we work hard to reach those standards. For me, that standard of a strong work ethic was set by my working-class parents.

When we don't meet those high standards, we're disappointed in ourselves and can't get past the feeling we could have done more. Pillar 4, Self-Compassion, points to discovering the magic dust in missing the mark.

While every pillar of *Graciously Assertive* offered an "aha moment," I owe a lot to Pillar 4 and to Dr. Davidds' clarity on how to redirect my actions. The experience was quite emotional, especially as I recognized other moments I could have done better not only for myself but those around me.

But then, I remembered Pillar 4 includes prioritizing self-forgiveness and self-care as a leader models the importance of well-being to their team. I learned the lesson of taking advantage of those moments and recognize them as a possibility. Without fear.

Isn't that the special safe space in which we want to live? A space that is filled with happy success for ourselves and those around us is the space we want to claim for ourselves as leaders.

In the California State Senate, bills that are the basis for new laws are submitted to the Appropriations Committee, a process that decides whether bills move forward or not. Recently, I submitted ten legislative bills I intended to pass. Our team was successful in passing nine bills from Appropriations. The one that did not pass happened to be very personal to me. I'm a survivor of domestic violence and the Chair of the Senate Select Committee on Domestic Violence. This bill extended the statute of limitations for victims to heal, come forward, and seek justice after experiencing horrific personal trauma. That was the one bill that died.

There was much success in the nine bills that passed, including a housing bill for those experiencing homelessness, a workforce development bill, and a bill named "Piqui's Law" that honors a young boy and reforms family court to ensure the courts are doing what's best for children.

And yet, because I was disappointed with losing that one bill, I could not celebrate the successful nine bills. I couldn't see past this one perceived failure.

The morning the bill passages were announced, a young female staff member approached me happily, praised our collective work, and exclaimed how well we had done. She said, "Senator, we did great! You are incredible. You passed nine bills. I'm so happy." But I couldn't give her that moment. I didn't allow her or us to celebrate because I was stuck on that one setback and dismissed her happiness and our accomplishments.

That moment was pivotal. I should have embraced her and told her how proud I was of the work we did and how proud I was that she was part of the success. I failed at that moment. I dismissed not only my work but lessened the value of her work. My own inability to get past that small setback derailed what should have been a celebratory uplifting moment.

What I realized when I read *Graciously Assertive* was I needed to pause in these moments. Actually, take a moment to reflect and understand that I don't need to be 100% perfect. As human beings, we want to succeed. As women, we don't give ourselves permission to fail. Dr. Davidds advises failure is a part of the journey and part of our growth. Learn the lesson, pick yourself up, and next time, do better, be better.

My epiphany was I didn't allow my staff member to have her moment of joy. I took that moment away from her. *Graciously Assertive* guided me to reflect, and I did, realizing I need to take moments of setbacks, learn from them, and do better.

This realization was transformative and inspirational because as much as I fell short in that moment, I was also able to recognize the many things I was doing right. That validation was heartwarming. This one experience transformed me to be a better human being and a better leader.

A few days after this event, I grabbed an available moment and redirected the staff to create an event to thank everyone, especially the young staff person I had dismissed, and celebrate her work and our accomplishment.

I hope everyone reading this book allows themselves to be vulnerable, allows themselves to fail once in a while, and allows themselves to celebrate even those small setbacks that are going to make us better in the future.

The 8 Pillars of Graciously Assertive Leadership work and create results. Dr. Davidds is a living example of how the system outlined in the book works. She is a prime example of someone who takes failures and deficiencies and forges them into successes. Her personal success is real and true. She was not born into success. In fact, she experienced a traumatic childhood and a difficult young adult life. However, she overcame the circumstances and succeeded. I felt while reading this book that if she could do it, I could do it, we all can do it.

We need to show women it's okay to be successful, and it's good to reach back and bring ten other women along with them. There's room for everyone at the top. We don't have to do it alone. This book offers a safe space for women who share their stories, making it okay to help other women and allow them to share resources and vulnerabilities.

We laugh when we hear a newborn baby doesn't come with operating instructions. Well, maybe the instruction manual is handed out during the time we spend as adults. Maybe *Graciously Assertive* is the book those in leadership roles may consider to be their memo to becoming better. Every reader will take away something incredibly powerful from it that they're able to implement in their own lives.

Leaders in the private and public sectors will also benefit from this book. Often, it's those who occupy the C-suites who need and can learn the most. This book will resonate with those at the top because they'll confront the fact that they're not perfect—none of us are. But, as Yasmin Davidds teaches us, as we move toward becoming better human beings, we become better leaders. The gift is learning to pay it forward and make sure others are growing with us.

This book redefined my belief that you don't have to be first and you don't have to be the best. You just have to be the best you, the best version of yourself. It's not about comparing yourself to others, it's about doing what's best for you.

Why wait for your successful life to find you? You can and you will find your success in life and on your chosen career path, and *Graciously Assertive: How Becoming a Better Human Being Makes You a Better Leader* offers the operating instructions to get started today.

State Senator Susan Rubio

INTRODUCTION

An Interaction between the Dalai Lama and Archbishop Tutu

A lot of people believe that for someone to be right, someone else has to be wrong, that two rights cannot coexist. However, the truth is what one person believes to be right is not necessarily better than what another person believes. Their beliefs might simply be different. Most importantly, one person can honor their own "right" while simultaneously honoring another person's "right."

The most beautiful example I have seen of this was in the Netflix documentary *Mission: Joy—Finding Happiness in Troubled Times*, which takes an in-depth look at the friendship between South African Archbishop Desmond Tutu and the 14th Dalai Lama, Gyalwa Rinpoche (or Tenzin Gyatso), and their efforts to live with joy in the face of adversity. In one scene, the Dalai Lama, a Buddhist, and Archbishop Tutu, an Anglican, traveled to Dharamsala, India, where approximately 2,500 children were gathered to celebrate the Dalai Lama's 80th birthday. His Holiness and the Archbishop were standing on stage when music began to play. Moved by the rhythm, Tutu began to sing and dance before reaching out and taking the Dalai Lama's hand in a warm invitation to join him. But as the Archbishop stood swinging their hands back and forth, the Dalai Lama remained calm, not singing or dancing because his deeply held Buddhist beliefs forbade such actions.

Instead of reacting negatively, the Dalai Lama responded in a way that demonstrated profound leadership. He allowed the Archbishop's joyous energy to flow through their joined hands while maintaining a smile that radiated his own profound love and understanding. He held space for his friend's jubilant expression without compromising his own commitment to his faith. The Archbishop's act transcended the boundaries of faith, embodying a leadership philosophy that resonates with authenticity and unity. In this moment, a powerful lesson was revealed: We can honor diverse perspectives without diminishing our own truths. Rather than imposing his own beliefs or inhibiting his friend's joy, the Dalai Lama embraced both elements in that wondrous moment. His actions reflected the essence of a true Graciously Assertive Leader, one who values others' expressions while upholding their own principles.

The heartwarming scene in *Mission* reveals a higher level of leadership perspective and demonstrates the importance of exuding grace, empathy, and the ability to foster unity amid diversity. It showcases the wisdom of holding space for others without sacrificing one's own core values. The Dalai Lama's instinctive response, devoid of ego or judgment, stands as an exquisite example of leadership that paves a way for unity through influence and respect. His example invites us to ponder the question: What would happen if we, as leaders, embraced differing viewpoints with the same open-heartedness? What if we created spaces for our team members to shine brightly while staying true to our own guiding principles? Just as the Dalai

Lama demonstrated, we can uphold our values and inspire those around us by embracing diverse perspectives without tearing anyone down. This story resonates as a call for leadership that transforms challenges into opportunities for connection. It illustrates that leadership isn't just about titles or authority; it's about weaving a tapestry of harmony and unity.

At its essence, Gracious Assertiveness encourages us to confidently advocate for ourselves while valuing alternative viewpoints. This fundamental principle paves the way for the transformation we aspire to achieve for ourselves and the world. As we collectively embrace this philosophy, we contribute to a vibrant tapestry of understanding, unity, and positive transformation.

A Call to Women Leaders to Ignite Your Inner Light

It is inherent within human beings to desire to make some form of difference in the world. And the truth is that each of us can make a difference by the decisions we make and the actions we take. Some of those changes are negative while others are positive, and even when we think we are sitting idly by and not making any waves of change at all, the very energy of life we hold within our hearts creates ripples that lead to change in some form. We have the power within us to control the changes we want to make and how we want to make them. Therefore, each of us should stand up, take notice, and ask ourselves, *What extraordinary mark do I wish to etch upon this world? How can I make positive changes that affect the world around me in the most practical and effective way? What bold vision fuels my journey as a human being?*

Over two decades ago, I embarked on a remarkable journey of crafting transformative women's leadership programs. At the heart of my endeavor was not only to refine the leadership skills of each participant but also to profoundly transform their spirit.

I envisioned a world where women didn't merely excel as traditional leaders but blossomed into the most exceptional versions of themselves. For me, the measure of my own success extended far beyond improving leadership competencies in others. It was intimately connected with my desire to elevate humanity and help shape a better world. Regardless of the financial outcomes of my initiatives, I considered my efforts a personal failure if they didn't contribute to a brighter world.

My purpose and legacy are grounded in nurturing women to become not only adept leaders but also confident individuals who carry a renewed sense of lightness in their spirits and have a profound connection to themselves and the world around them. For me, this epitomizes genuine success. Achieving this lofty goal requires the shedding of the burdens of past traumas and limiting beliefs and replacing them with the warmth of a supportive community, empowered beliefs, and an unwavering commitment to living authentically. I firmly believe the journey toward becoming a better leader and, more importantly, a better human being is anchored in living authentically, facing truths head-on, and embracing the healing power of love that spurs growth. This is the philosophy that breathes life into my work, fueling its potential to create lasting change.

So, to all the women out there who want more from their lives, I extend an invitation to ponder the depth of your own aspirations. As you seek to excel as leaders, remember your journey encompasses the very essence of your humanity. By embracing authenticity, shedding the weight of the past, and cultivating a heart imbued with compassion, you not only elevate your leadership but also illuminate the path toward a brighter, more connected world.

Letting your inner light shine has the power to transform you as a woman as well as make significant changes in the world around you.

CHAPTER ONE

BECOMING A BETTER LEADER BEGINS WITH BECOMING A BETTER HUMAN BEING

It hit me like a wrecking ball. At a critical juncture in my career, I was working with a coach, trying to understand what was most important for me to focus on as I sought clarity for next steps in my business and life. As I spoke, I realized that everything I mentioned indicated that emotional or psychological safety was at the core of everything I did. Up until that moment I hadn't realized that my entire life, being, and career had been built with the intention of creating safe spaces. My coach asked me to envision what psychological safety looked like to me.

"What did it look like when you were a child?" she asked.

As I probed for an answer, trying to envision what that intangible aspect looked like for me, I realized that I had no memory, vision, or sense of safety from the household I grew up in. My father was an alcoholic and a destructive force in my life, so I experienced no sense of physical safety or psychological safety. I was always in survival mode.

I told my coach that the first time I felt safe was when I entered rehab with a methamphetamine addiction in 1993 at the age of 23. Life had gotten so bad for me I no longer cared to live, and methamphetamines were the only thing getting me out of bed and allowing me to function every day. However, they inevitably took a great toll on me, and after eleven months of using them day after day to get up and go to school at the University of Southern California (USC), study, and work three jobs on campus, I couldn't do it anymore.

I tried to get off methamphetamines on my own, but every time I did, my body ached, and an overwhelming sense of anxiety and depression overwhelmed me. I ended up returning to my dependency just to function and survive, but the day finally came when I could no longer do it. I no longer cared to do it. Unfortunately, my body was addicted to the drug, and I did not know what to do. Desperate, and seeing no other choice, I decided the only way to free myself was to commit suicide. I was driving along the 101 freeway in Los Angeles by Universal Studios, contemplating my desperate situation, when I veered off the Universal City Drive exit and went straight to a pay phone.

The fear and finality of taking my own life had overtaken me. I desperately needed help but didn't know who to call. I had already tried reaching out to social services, but they told me I couldn't enter rehab because I wasn't under eighteen or pregnant. So, there I was in the middle of my predicament, penniless and alone. I tried to get a loan, but no one was willing to accommodate me because I was a student with no collateral. I even tried calling a suicide hotline a few times, but they merely gave me thirty minutes of their time before sending me on my way.

There was one exception. On one of the suicide prevention calls, a kind-hearted crisis counselor named Laura spoke with me. She was so understanding, and she tried her best to comfort me. At the end of our conversation, she told me, "I know I'm not supposed to do this, but I'm going to give you my home number. If you ever need anything, call me." I had written her number down on a little piece of paper and tucked it in my wallet for safekeeping, never thinking I would use it. But when that day came, and I decided I no longer wanted to live, I stood at the pay phone, desperately searching for that piece of paper in my wallet, hoping maybe, just maybe, there was something she could do to save me.

It was six in the morning on a Thursday when I called Laura. As soon as she picked up the phone, I anxiously whispered, "Laura, I don't care to live anymore. I want to die." I paused and waited for a response, but when I heard nothing, I continued, "You don't know me, but we had a thirty-minute suicide intervention phone session a few months ago. You gave me your home number and told me to call you if I ever needed anything."

Finally, she broke her silence. "I have been teaching yoga classes every Thursday morning at 6:00 a.m. for seven years," she said. "I have never missed a session. I know I set my alarm clock last night, but it didn't go off this morning. I'm supposed to be here for you. Don't move. Tell me where you are. I'm going to come get you."

True to her word, Laura arrived and took me to the Beverly Hills Women's Clinic, where we sat for eight hours, searching for a rehab facility that would take me on a loan basis. We finally found one. It was called First Step, located in Laguna Beach. The requirement for me to go to this rehabilitation center was to take out a loan I would have to repay over time, as well as provide a cash payment I would need to come up with within two weeks after entering rehab. I didn't know how I was going to get the sum, but I agreed to do it out of desperation. I needed to get in because I was at the end of my rope. I didn't want to think that far ahead and convinced myself I would figure out a way.

Once the arrangements were made, the staff at the rehab said they wouldn't be able to take me for a few days. I didn't know what to expect, and I was petrified. The night before I was to enter, I repeatedly threw up from the anxiety. Like a frightened kid, I asked my mom if I could sleep with her that night, and she lovingly agreed. I told her I was going to rehab, but she really didn't understand what I was talking about. In her mind, I was going to Laguna Beach for some sort of vacation.

The next morning, my sister drove me to the rehab center and dropped me off. Much to my surprise, it was a beautiful six-bedroom home in the hills of Laguna Beach surrounded by breathtaking scenery. However, the beauty of the place barely subdued my anxiety. When I walked in, I asked the admission counselor, "How long is it going to take to fix me? I have things to do, people to see, places to go, so I need to do this quickly."

The lady smiled and said, "You don't have to stay here. You can leave anytime you want, but if you're going to stay, you need to surrender and be committed to the process."

Surrender? I thought to myself. *What the heck does surrender mean?* My first reaction was to bolt for the door, but I felt I had no choice but to do as she said. I failed trying to get clean on my own, and I knew I needed help. I didn't know how this would be different, but I knew I had to try. The moment I left the admissions room and walked into the living room where the other residents were gathered, a sense of peace washed over me. Everyone immediately embraced me and accepted me. There were no judgments, no pretenses, and no social status. It didn't matter where you came from, how much money you made, or what your ethnicity was. There was only love.

There were no judgments, no pretenses, and no social status. It didn't matter where you came from, how much money you made, or what your ethnicity was. There was only love.

We were all there for a common purpose, our own survival, so everyone in that home did what we could to help each other realize that goal. We needed to physically heal from our addictions and emotionally heal from the pain that drove us to use in the first place.

During that first night, something magical happened to me. I hadn't been able to sleep an entire night for months, only sleeping about three or four hours. But that night, I slept 12 fabulous hours. I went into a deep, peaceful sleep I had never experienced before, and I realized—for the very first time—that I felt safe.

The next thirty days in rehab completely transformed my life as well as my career trajectory. I had finally found a home in which I felt emotionally, physically, sexually, and spiritually safe. I found a family who loved me unconditionally and didn't want to hurt me. I was no longer alone. In that house, we all had a common purpose and vision. It didn't matter if you were a CEO who was there for alcoholism or a homeless sixteen-year-old kid. Status was irrelevant. What mattered was we were all there to get better, to get clean, to stay alive, and to heal. Each of us began to figure out why we became addicted in the first place, and how we could live clean lives from that point onward.

We accomplished this difficult task by being one other's mirror of truth from a place of love and compassion. We studied and attended meetings together every day. We worked on the twelve-step program. We broke bread. We laughed, we cried, we became strong together. And when one of us became weak or one of us hurt with pain, we would all be there to embrace, love, and support them because we knew one day it would be our turn. We would stumble, fall, and have a bad day, but we had our tribe—that community of love to support us.

Two weeks into rehab, the time came for me to make the cash payment, or I would have to leave. Of course, I hadn't found a way to come up with the money, and I was devastated because I was not ready to leave. I knew I couldn't stay clean on my own, and I was not strong enough yet. Just when I was beginning to collapse into despair, a miracle happened. As I was packing my things, my counselor entered with a small box that had arrived in the mail for me. I curiously opened it, and inside I found some candy, chocolate, and a white envelope. The package was from a college friend, who had spent the summer in Europe, so we had been disconnected for a few months. He knew I had been going through hard times but didn't know the extent of it. Upon his return from Europe, he reached out and called my home. My mother told him I was on vacation in Laguna Beach and gave him the address of the rehab.

He had no idea what I was going through, and he had no idea I needed to come up with money to stay in rehab. However, something compelled him to send me a few snacks he knew I loved and cash in the envelope with a note that read, "Just in case you need anything." It was the exact amount of money I needed to stay in rehab! I broke into tears, hurried to my counselor, and told him what had just happened.

He replied, "Girl, get on your knees and thank God because this is a miracle!"

And it truly was. There was no way my friend could have known about the urgent financial need I had, yet somehow he was able to help me. And that wasn't the only time something amazing like that happened to me. Through the grace of God, miracles like this have happened throughout my life. There have been numerous angels who have blessed me with their presence, their gifts, and their love. Because of my friend's generosity, I was able to stay for a few additional weeks, becoming stronger and preparing to face the world again with renewed hope. And in those four weeks I spent in rehab, I became a better person and a better human being, and I vowed that anything I did afterward would be done in a spirit of community.

It was when I shared this story with my coach that I came to a stark realization that the safety I experienced in rehab was necessary for effective and transformative leadership development. Everything good, everything transformative, everything that makes us better human beings starts with a feeling of psychological safety. I had created what I longed for and needed so much without even knowing it, and I realized how powerful our subconscious is. Then I realized what a badass I was! For the last 20 years, I had been creating entrepreneur ventures that gave me and others what we so desperately needed: psychological safety.

What Is Psychological Safety?

In a nutshell, psychological safety is the state in which an individual can open up and express themselves without fear of judgment or reprisal. This type of atmosphere is generally found in close and intimate relationships, in which those involved trust and accept each other, giving the benefit of doubt in situations that are deemed questionable. Psychological safety is a critical part of emotional health and healing. For this reason, it is both encouraged and emphasized by therapists and executive coaches when dealing with individuals struggling with challenging life situations.

My Multicultural Women Executive Leadership Program (MWELP) provides women from all walks of life with a safe environment in which to heal, thrive, and remove self-limitations, so they can become the best versions of themselves. These courses offer women a sanctuary where they can come to recover, flourish, and break free from limitations that are holding them back from unleashing their true potential. My program offers them a launch pad from which they can embark on their journey to become empowered instead of weak or hindered by characteristic flaws that are more often than not programed into their psyches by the world around them.

Those of us within the institute are more than just a community. We are family. Everyone involved, my students, the leadership team, alumni, and advisors, are all part of this extended family. I am fully committed to their well-being, as they are to mine and to one another's, and this commitment endures across time. I honor and embrace them all for who they are, recognizing that each one of them is on their own unique journey. Judgment has no place in this environment. If one woman insists on judging another, she is kindly asked to leave the program. There is no condemnation. We release her with love and extend an open invitation for her to return when she feels ready to make a positive change toward empowerment of herself and others.

However, the MWELP did not start this way. It began as a traditional leadership development program launched in partnership with the USC Marshall School of Business. Organizations had hired me as an executive coach and organizational development consultant to help them develop women in leadership, particularly women of color. In my work with these organizations, I had one-on-one conversations with women in an attempt to identify the reasons behind why they felt stuck, and what was limiting their leadership development. I soon discovered the vast majority of them did not feel as though they could freely express themselves due to limitations imposed on them at work, home, and even by themselves. They just didn't feel safe enough to discuss their true feelings for fear of being overheard, judged, and ridiculed. These women were afraid to express themselves honestly, and even if they did make an attempt at an honest reply, they felt they were sharing too much information. Sometimes they felt structural and systemic issues were holding them back, and at times, they even struggled to speak to me freely.

As I sat in the boardrooms and conference rooms to interview these women, I realized even in those spaces they didn't feel free to speak openly and honestly. I wanted to enable them to share their struggles, identify their obstacles, and build the foundation needed to foster community. Having gone through my own transformation of healing and growth, learning to feel safe enough to talk and share, I felt I could help these women give their experiences a voice, to understand their reality, and overcome their obstacles. The process was truly revolutionary, transformational, and validating, and I wanted to share it with as many women as possible.

I began to consider what I could do to make a difference for more than one woman at a time. To solve the issue of safe spaces and help greater numbers of women, I determined the best way to proceed was to create a program and have organizations send their women leaders and leadership prospects to me. I would take it upon myself to create the safe spaces required for them to share their struggles and identify their obstacles, and together we would forge a strong community together. I would not only help them build the self-esteem and confidence they required but arm them with tools needed to positively affect their surroundings and build their own communities.

As I was building the foundations of this idea, I recalled my own journey through rehab and its support community, which led to my transformation, healing, and growth and later to a radical enhancement of my leadership abilities. I recalled most clearly how I felt safe enough to talk about my experiences in front of others. I had learned that the crucial step is to give our experiences a voice in order to experience healing and growth. When we say our pains and struggles aloud, they become real and not simply something existing within the confused, depressed recesses of our minds. Not only does speaking freely help us to identify core issues but it also strengthens us and allows others to validate our experiences by saying, "Oh my gosh! I'm going through the same thing!" Free expression and validation are powerful keys in the evolutionary process of transformation.

Not only does speaking freely help us to identify core issues but it also strengthens us and allows others to validate our experiences by saying, "Oh my gosh! I'm going through the same thing!" Free expression and validation are powerful keys in the evolutionary process of transformation.

In 2001, I embarked on what would become my life's mission. After much research in the area of women's development and empowerment, I wrote and released my first book, *Empowering Latinas: Breaking Boundaries, Freeing Lives*. As the message spread, it catapulted into a movement within

Latino communities, not only in the United States but also worldwide. With my mission to empower Latinas everywhere clearly defined, I began traveling the world on speaking tours for companies, nonprofit organizations, colleges, universities, and government agencies. My goal was to equip Latinas with the resources to overcome personal and cultural obstacles, take control of their lives, and live life on their own terms.

To my surprise, and much to my excitement, I became an institution of sorts, catching the attention of Venezuelan investors who would become my business partners in launching unique products and services catering to the Latino market worldwide. As my business grew, so did my personal brand. I became the go-to Latina talent development expert for corporations and organizations throughout the United States.

Soon after, I crossed over from solely serving the Latina community to the empowerment and development of all women. I then published another book, titled *Take Back Your Power: How to Reclaim It, Keep It, and Use It to Get What You Deserve.* My area of expertise expanded to the executive development of women, especially multicultural women, as I consulted for hundreds of corporations and academic institutions, creating women's leadership development programs.

One day, the founder and CEO of a leading negotiation company approached me, asking if I could assist in the expansion of the company's Latin American market by training and developing corporate men and women in the art of negotiation. Accepting the challenge, I became one of the leading Latina female negotiation experts in the United States and Latin America, training thousands of corporate leaders in more than two hundred blue-chip companies, including Apple, Microsoft, ExxonMobil, JPMorgan Chase, Coca-Cola, and

General Electric, in twenty-two countries—Argentina, Chile, Peru, Bolivia, UK, Spain, Brazil, Mexico, Paraguay, and more.

In 2011, following a deep dive into gender negotiation, I launched the Women's Institute of Negotiation, the only organization of its kind in the world, dedicated to the teaching, instruction, and development of women's negotiating skills and business expertise. The Women's Institute of Negotiation utilizes gender-based negotiation simulations, case studies, discussion, and individualized coaching to provide women with experiential negotiation training. It also partnered with the UCSD Rady School of Management to launch the Women's Negotiation and Leadership Certificate Program, which features three curated courses and has awarded thousands of women accredited certification upon completion. My fourth book, *Your Own Terms: A Woman's Guide to Taking Charge of Any Negotiation*, comprises the core curriculum for the program. It teaches and emphasizes essential negotiating and leadership skills to help women discover their natural strengths, gain confidence, and enhance their roles in their organizations.

This all culminated in 2013, when I founded the Dr. Yasmin Davidds Leadership Institute and developed the first-ever Latina Global Executive Leadership Program and Latina Entrepreneur Program in partnership with the USC Marshall School of Business. The practices and principles I teach are used to transform women from all walks of life into successful Graciously Assertive leaders. As women participate, they learn to share strategies and principles and to conduct themselves in a way that enables them to break through barriers. The result is validation and empowerment.

We learned quickly that this empowerment and self-advocation, when not tempered with Gracious Assertiveness, had an effect opposite of the one intended.[1]

Power—empowerment—comes with the responsibility of delivery. To be truly effective and powerful requires appropriate, responsible communication. It requires being a better human and transmitting the right energy because our energy and our behavior impact others. This is where the foundational leadership principles—being socially aware (understanding how behavior and emotions affect others) and self-regulation (adjusting our behavior for our intended impact)—come in. They allow us to become more effective and thoughtful as communicators and leaders.

Power—empowerment—comes with the responsibility of delivery. To be truly effective and powerful requires appropriate, responsible communication.

What began as a traditional leadership program to create safe spaces for women has now manifested as the Multicultural Women Executive Leadership Program. It has grown organically, with phenomenal results. Not surprisingly, a large body of leadership development research supports our ideals.

A study called "Taking Gender into Account: Theory and Design for Women's Leadership Development Programs" demonstrates how women's leadership development is not only about learning competencies but requires transformative identity work.[2] The underlying principles of Graciously Assertive Leadership validate the fact that when a woman sees herself as a leader and a human being, transformation begins in earnest. Through the program, we help women make the shift from who they thought they were to who they can become, who they truly are!

However, it is no secret: Strong females are often disliked.[3] Through my program, I had to find ways to teach women to self-advocate and communicate graciously, so they could be respected and well-liked and achieve success. Gracious Assertiveness requires balance and is key to a woman's effectiveness in leadership. The inspirational, moral leader is what new leadership organizations are seeking. It is all about reaching bigger visions, bigger goals, bigger objectives, and the Graciously Assertive methodology is leading the way with the 8 Pillars of the Graciously Assertive Communication style.

Most recently, I was tasked by the chancellor's office of the California community colleges, which consists of 1.8 million students in 116 colleges—the largest system of higher education in the United States and third largest in the world—to create and launch a Women's Equity Empowerment Leadership Certificate Program for faculty, administrators, and staff. As a leadership expert, I continue to work in-depth with organizations—coaching leaders, training executives, and effecting positive change from the top down as well as the bottom up. I train Fortune 500 executives in the merging of diverse corporate cultures and also guide corporate, non-profit, and governmental teams in crucial negotiations.

All the hard work makes me immensely grateful for the opportunities afforded to me, for the successes of women leaders who have been empowered and developed through my programs, and for the accolades awarded to me by the U.S. Congress, the California State Senate, and the California State Assembly, which bring to light the positive impact empowered women leaders have on business, education, and the economy.

CHAPTER TWO

BEING GRACIOUS, ASSERTIVE, AND LIVING THE 8 PILLARS

Before we dive into the 8 Pillars that make up Graciously Assertive Leaders, we need to define the terms *gracious*, *assertive*, and *Graciously Assertive* so we are all together in our understanding of the premise. The Merriam-Webster Dictionary defines *graciousness* as being "marked by kindness, courtesy." However, for me, graciousness goes beyond being kind; it involves a spirit of gratitude to all the people who cross your path. It is a loving energy, and it's tangible—you can feel it. It's kindness but deeper, a belief that we are all connected as human beings. We all deserve to be treated with respect, and we all deserve to be heard.

Graciousness also boasts a spiritual component of connection, of humanity. It is profoundly deep and personal and cannot exist without love, kindness, warmth, and compassion. At its roots, graciousness is kindness and courtesy, even if we don't feel so deep and spiritual. If we see graciousness as kindness, we can still be Graciously Assertive Communicators by simply being kind whenever we chose to assert ourselves.

Some may think that graciousness and assertiveness aren't really compatible. The Merriam-Webster Dictionary defines *assertiveness* as being "characterized by bold or confident statements and behavior." In other words, boldly expressing ourselves is assertiveness. When we think of boldness, we often think of directness, harshness. But that is why graciousness is so important; we can be direct, bold, and confident while also being kind and warm. As we move through this book, we'll meet students who have made the transformation, as well as leaders who demonstrate the Graciously Assertive mindset every day.

Levels of Gracious Assertiveness

There are three levels of Gracious Assertiveness:

- A Graciously Assertive Communication style
- A Graciously Assertive Leadership style
- A Graciously Assertive Lifestyle

Let's compare this to a three-story building. At **Level One** is a Graciously Assertive Communication style. At this level, you communicate graciously to be effective and achieve your goal.

If you want to create a win-win scenario in a conversation, communicating with a Graciously Assertive style will help you reach that goal. The gracious part of this communication style is kindness and empathy. When you are kind and empathetic with others, it allows them to open themselves up to listening to you. They have no need to be defensive as they can feel your warmth and kindness. However, you should never have to do this at the cost of being direct, honest, and firm when needed.

For example, a partner was asked to produce a book of instructions for one of my events. The paper she chose to complete the assignment was of very low quality, and I was unhappy with the results. How did I approach this matter? Simple. I began by acknowledging that she had put effort into getting this task completed, and I was appreciative of her effort.

I then mentioned the areas in which she did very well, primarily the book's layout and the effectiveness it had on those who read it.

Next, I explained my perspective with clarity and respect, pointing out the quality of the paper she had chosen for the project was not up to par. I continued by asking her to ensure that the same quality of paper is not used again for any of our projects and, more specifically, not for a book we're passing out to our audience or clients. I asked her to use paper quality three levels higher, so she would clearly understand my expectations and the need for better results. She later shared with me that she was very grateful for the grace I offered her, saying it inspired her to want to do better.

It is a simple example, but it illustrates my point. Tempering assertiveness with kindness and empathy is crucial to fostering healthy communication.

Level Two is a Graciously Assertive Leadership style. Most often, it entails gathering others around your vision as leader and bringing that vision to fruition. This vision often involves how you want to move an organization or a department or even a team to reach a certain goal. These leaders will reverse engineer to determine what it will take to get there as well as how they can inspire and help their people drive their actions toward the fulfillment of their vision.

Graciously Assertive Leaders have figured out the best way to influence a person or group of people is to show they care about each individual. Research shows the greatest source of influence a person can use is empathy, because empathy builds trust.[4] If people are going to follow you as a leader, you have to build trust.

A Graciously Assertive Leader empathizes with the people they lead, actively listening to them and simultaneously holding them accountable. Graciousness and assertiveness together help them inspire those they lead; in turn their teams become invested. It becomes a mutually beneficial relationship in which everyone wins!

The pillars include self-awareness, social awareness (awareness of others), self-regulation, self-love (self-compassion), gratitude, zero tolerance for judgment (nonjudgmental), healthy boundaries, and Graciously Assertive communication. Each of these pillars has the potential to enhance your personal growth as well as your leadership abilities. When you embody these pillars, you can live a Graciously Assertive Lifestyle with ease, be a better human, and develop into a great leader.

Let's explore the 8 Pillars of Graciously Assertive Leadership together.

1. SELF-AWARENESS

Self-awareness is about being aware of the way you feel and the impact your feelings can have on decisions, behavior, and performance. People who are self-aware are conscious of the role their feelings can play in these areas and are better equipped to manage this influence effectively.

Self-awareness is pivotal for understanding our strengths, weaknesses, and motivations. It requires embracing our unique story and acknowledging our inner strength, leading to a deeper understanding of ourselves. Self-awareness empowers us to make well-informed decisions, have greater self-confidence, and achieve personal growth.

Not surprisingly, self-awareness is the number one competency of emotional intelligence. They go hand in hand when it comes to the powerful and positive Graciously Assertive Leadership style. We have to be aware not only of our strengths but also of our weaknesses, as well as how our life experiences impact who we are as leaders (or potential leaders). Self-awareness also requires that we be clear on what we value, live in alignment with those values, and understand the significance of our values.

Why are values crucial to self-awareness? As leaders, we are under constant observation, held accountable by those around us. It is crucial that we first understand our own values and beliefs before we can effectively guide others. Therefore, we must lead ourselves first. Self-awareness empowers us to lead authentically because we know ourselves so well. We know what affects us, positively and negatively. We know how to get around negative energy, how to make informed choices, and make sound business decisions. We are able to understand and instill confidence in our team, because they know that we know ourselves. They see us as self-confident and self-assured because of our self-awareness.

2. SOCIAL AWARENESS

Next up in our pillars is social awareness, that is, a mindfulness of how our energy and our behavior impacts others.

As I mentioned previously, empathy and understanding are foundational components of Graciously Assertive Leadership. As leaders, we must recognize the uniqueness of each of our team members' journeys. Social awareness allows us to establish meaningful connections with each member of our team. Although we are all equal, we cannot treat each team member we are leading in the same way. Individuals have different needs, and equity is about giving every person what they need.

Although we are all equal, we cannot treat each team member we are leading in the same way. Individuals have different needs, and equity is about giving every person what they need.

If we speak to everybody the same way, knowing different people need to hear things in different ways in order to really hear, we are sharing a message equally but we're not building equity. In this scenario, only half of them will get the message, and the rest of them won't, because they don't hear messages the same way. We aren't really presenting the message in the way they need to hear it in order to be effective. When we present the message in ways they can hear it, we are building equity.

Our heightened awareness of others fosters compassion in us and in others, enabling us to tailor our leadership approach to individual needs, thus cultivating trust and stronger relationships.

Social awareness breeds empathy and understanding for those around us, so we can recognize each team member's unique journey and connect with them more meaningfully. Connection is key for success.

3. SELF-REGULATION

Self-regulation is a crucial component of Graciously Assertive Leadership. It is our ability to effectively manage our emotions. Self-regulation, also known as self-management, is among the top three most important elements of emotional intelligence. Self-regulation not only encompasses our ability to manage our emotions but also our capacity to influence our team's emotional environment.

Self-regulation not only encompasses our ability to manage our emotions but also our capacity to influence our team's emotional environment.

Self-regulation allows us to consciously shape our emotional responses and set an example of emotional maturity. This then fosters smoother interactions, effective counsel, resolutions, and a positive work atmosphere. In other words, self-regulation leads to staff regulation.

For example, I once had an employee who did not meet the mark on a task. I had to be mindful to be sensitive to her because we were in a group meeting. One of my strengths is empathy, so I was able to empathize and put myself in her position. I knew she would want to be told what she needed to do better, but also I knew I had to be kind in my delivery.

If I was frustrated or tired, my message could come across as rude. In the meeting, I had to self-regulate—that is, I had to be thoughtful about how I spoke and acted—to ensure I continued to inspire my team and guide them toward success.

The first three pillars—self-awareness, social awareness, and self-regulation—go hand in hand. Why? Self-awareness is our perception not only of our strengths and weaknesses, but also our motivations. Social awareness is our awareness of others but also describes our awareness of how we impact others. Self-regulation comes into play in both areas, guiding us to effectively manage our emotions and, in doing so, positively influence those around us.

After seven years of working as a consultant and negotiation instructor for the leading global negotiation training company in the world, I had taught negotiation skills to thousands of Fortune 500 executives in the United States, Latin America, and Mexico. I excelled at it. No one had ever challenged my competency until the day I walked into the boardroom of a large country club in Mexico to teach a negotiation course to eighteen male executives, each at least twice my age.

When I entered the room, they were clearly expecting someone else.

"Buenos días, Señorita," one of the men said. "Where is the negotiation instructor? Are you his secretary?"

I smiled, responding amiably but confidently. "Hello. No, gentlemen, I am the negotiation instructor."

From the looks on their faces, I could tell they thought I was joking. Chuckling, they asked disbelievingly, "Where is the negotiation instructor?"

Once again, I smiled, confident. "Seriously gentlemen," I said firmly. "I *am* the instructor."

The men looked at each other incredulously, their faces reflecting astonishment and disappointment. To them, my identity as a woman discredited me. Due to my gender, I needed to call on my expertise and emphasize my credibility and competence.

I struggled not to squirm under their scrutiny. I estimated I had five minutes to prove I was more competent in the art of negotiation than they were.

I stood tall, shoulders squared. "Gentlemen," I said, "please take a seat so I can share a little about my work." I then did something I would never do with female executives: I bragged. I flaunted my negotiation style, adapting to the way men communicate. I explained how I enhanced the negotiation skills of thousands of executive-level professionals in several world-famous companies. As the name-dropping began, their mouths dropped in awe. They were beginning to respect and accept me.

I continued to share more names of powerful executives I had worked with in Argentina, Chile, Colombia, Paraguay, and Honduras. They were impressed, but I couldn't stop yet. I needed their 100 percent commitment so they would be open to learning. I continued "bragging" for fifteen minutes, listing my accomplishments, accolades, and expertise, and finally won over their respect. Had I done the same with a group of women, I'd be the most hated person in the room, but the men respected me because of it, and that respect crossed over into a multitude of business ventures and deep, decades-long friendships.

Ten years prior, before my practice of the emotional intelligence Graciously Assertive Pillars of self-awareness, social awareness, and self-regulation, I would have been insulted, let my emotions get the better of me, and responded starkly, ultimately derailing my objective of developing these gentlemen into better negotiators. Self-awareness afforded me the understanding needed to make value-based decisions in the moment. I knew as a strong young Latina, the odds were stacked against me in the male-dominated world of negotiation. Plus,

I was in Guadalajara, Mexico, where a strong "machismo" stems from longstanding traditional values. I used my knowledge to help me pivot toward my objective.

Social awareness allowed me to see how I navigated the scenario that would determine my success or failure. In my earlier years, I would have been annoyed by the men's underestimation and responded with sarcasm or defensiveness. Instead, I saw the humor in it and used bragging as my strategy.

Furthermore, self-regulation helped me keep my emotions under control. I could've reacted with annoyance, impatience, or even anger. But, by self-regulating, I decided to approach the situation with a light heart. I strategically repositioned myself to resonate with my audience and did so without compromising my values.

4. SELF-COMPASSION

The fourth pillar of Graciously Assertive Leadership is self-compassion. It is our ability to treat ourselves kindly, respectfully, and most importantly, with love. To many, loving oneself might seem narcissistic. But that couldn't be further from the truth. Radiating self-love positively influences our interactions because when we love ourselves, we are able to love others. Demonstrating that self-compassion should be actively encouraged to cultivate a culture of well-being within our teams.

Senator Rubio talked a great deal about this pillar and the importance of self-care, self-forgiveness, and self-compassion. It is when we care for our body and soul, and prioritize our personal well-being, that we are able to foster a healthy and safe space for our team members. Just think about it. If we dislike—or even loathe—ourselves, we will inevitably exude this negative energy to the people around us.

Self-compassion is therefore necessary if we wish to build a flourishing team and community. It includes forgiving and caring for ourselves, body and soul, so we can radiate love to others.

Self-compassion is therefore necessary if we wish to build a flourishing team and community. It includes forgiving and caring for ourselves, body and soul, so we can radiate love to others.

One Friday, a colleague, Samantha, received an email from a client asking about a weekly report. Realizing she had forgotten to create and send it, Samantha quickly pulled it together and sent it over, apologizing for the oversight. The client was kind and understanding, but Samantha could not stop criticizing herself. She had quickly fallen into her old habit of self-criticizing for her mistakes when she recalled what she had recently learned from the 8 Pillars. She decided to stop berating herself for the mistake and apply what she had learned about self-compassion.

Samantha began by taking hold of her critical internal thoughts so she would not spiral into negativity. Yes, she had made a mistake and a critical thought followed, but this time she viewed it as just that—a critical thought—and acknowledged it. While she felt frustrated by her mistake, she knew that in identifying the feeling, she was taking the first step toward being compassionate.

Samantha then considered how she extended compassion readily to others but not herself and realized she needed to give herself more grace. She thought, *I made a mistake, just as others do on a regular basis. My client extended compassion and kindness to me, and I need to do the same.* With her thoughts turned toward self-compassion, Samantha felt the self-loathing and self-criticism begin to fade.

Finally, she realized that she needed to move forward—the critical and final component of self-compassion. She knew she didn't want to forget the report for her clients and sought a solution to avoid the mistake in the future. She created a checklist for the week's end and put a reminder in her calendar to review client reports and ensure everyone had what they needed. In extending some grace to herself, rather than self-criticizing, she was able to develop a positive solution which benefited her, her coworkers, and her clients.

5. GRATITUDE

Next in our list of pillars is gratitude, which the Merriam-Webster Dictionary defines as the "state of being grateful or thankful for something or someone." It entails focusing on the positive and finding the value in all of life's moments—even the moments that are challenging. Adopting a grateful mindset can help us inspire our teams to focus on the positive in challenging experiences. Guiding our teams with optimism through difficulties ultimately builds resilience and helps them become more adaptable. It also fosters growth, innovation, and a more positive environment.

We cannot be Graciously Assertive without a gratitude mindset. It is impossible because graciousness comes from kindness, and we have to tap into our kindness to succeed. We have to have a sense of gratitude. As we approach team members, we can foster a mindset of gratitude by asking, "What has this person done lately for which I can show appreciation? What am I grateful for about this person before I communicate with them?" This allows us to approach others with kindness, and without kindness, we cannot be gracious. Gratitude is key, and it applies to all the various aspects of leadership and life.

Today, I live my life from a place of gratitude, though this has not always been my practice. Like the other pillars, it is one which has to be fully embraced because it is impossible to live a Graciously Assertive lifestyle without gratitude. Graciousness comes from kindness, and in order to be genuinely kind, we need to be grateful. But how?

Graciousness comes from kindness, and in order to be genuinely kind, we need to be grateful.

I began by approaching team members and asking myself, *What am I grateful for about this person?* This allowed me to have a renewed perspective of each of the individuals on my team and to recognize just how much they improve my life. Ultimately, by embracing a gratitude mentality, I was able to become a more positive, thoughtful, and considerate person and leader.

6. ZERO TOLERANCE FOR JUDGMENT

Inclusive leadership thrives on a judgment-free environment. As Graciously Assertive Leaders, our active rejection of judgment creates a safe space for team members to express themselves freely. This full-on inclusivity fosters collaborative and diverse team dynamics, sparking innovation and collective growth.

Zero tolerance for judgment is crucial to creating a psychologically safe space for our teams. If people feel they're going to be judged, they cannot feel safe. Judgment and safety do not—and cannot—coexist because judgment instills fear. Research shows that having zero tolerance for judgment creates thriving businesses.[5]

Psychological safety cannot exist if team members feel they do not belong in the group or are outsiders. It is here that Pillar 6, having zero tolerance for judgment, comes into play. In order to protect team members from feeling excluded, my client Carrie, a director in a pharmaceutical company, instituted a zero tolerance for judgment within her team. She defined judgment as interactions that caused anyone to feel disadvantaged, excluded, diminished, or deflated. Together, as a team, they determined what the policy looked like and implemented the following:

- Education on unconscious biases and recognizing how they may be manifesting biases within the team;
- The creation of shared identity and shared goals, thus exploring the intersectionality of the individuals on the team;
- Exposure on how team members have felt different or judged throughout their lives in order to provide insight on the struggles each person has faced; and
- Discussion of sensitive subjects, shining a light on issues normally swept under the rug and creating a feeling of common humanity and compassion.

Not only did Carrie institute a zero-tolerance policy within her team, she also embraced the policy in her life, living by her personal standards of nonjudgment and staying away from people who indulge judging others. She confessed it has been the greatest gift she could have given herself, bringing her a life of inner peace.

7. HEALTHY BOUNDARIES

Effective leaders need to set healthy boundaries. This fosters a work-life balance, guards against burnout, but also helps guide our employees to set healthy boundaries themselves.

In doing so, we have to ensure we are gracious, kind, and supportive while also firm and assertive. It is important to be kind and equally important to establish your boundaries and ascertain that they are respected.

For example, if you are among my employees, I expect you to be at work at 8 a.m. It is what we agreed on, so you shouldn't show up at 9 or 9:30. I'm depending on you to do the calculations in terms of how long it's going to take you to get from home to work, what you're going to have to do to get there, and then for you to deliver on a daily basis. You have to factor in the things you can control and even the things you can't because that is the expectation. If you can't do that, I don't know if I can work with you. It is often a hard conversation, but to be a Graciously Assertive Communicator, you must be firm and direct and set healthy boundaries.

But remember, I didn't say I was going to fire you. What I said was true—I don't think I can work with you because you are not giving me what I need or meeting my expectations. It's then up to you to make the decision. You have to figure it out. If you choose to go somewhere else, it's better that I know that now rather than later. If you say, "Oh, my God! I understand. There's a mutual obligation. This person was supportive, supported me and invested in my career, and I need to be relentless and hold up my end of the bargain," then great! Both of us can move forward—together.

Pillar 7 does not only require us to set healthy boundaries but it also asks us to model and encourage team members to do the same. Boundaries allow us to foster mutual respect and contribute to a healthy work-life balance. They are also essential to Graciously Assertive leadership. Why? I've learned from experience and the testimonies of other leaders that if we lean too much toward graciousness, those around us may take advantage and not put forth the effort needed to create success. Healthy boundaries, however, allow us to assert ourselves, draw a line, and establish discipline—in ourselves and others.

8. **GRACIOUSLY ASSERTIVE COMMUNICATION**

Graciously Assertive Communication is the final pillar. It is the ability to communicate in a way that is firm and direct yet kind and respectful of the feelings and needs of others. Cultivating this communication style empowers us to foster an open dialogue and encourages team members to voice their truth.

For example, my client Sara took control of her work-life balance at work by setting healthy boundaries and utilizing the Graciously Assertive Communication Model (GACM). Her position, managing large, global teams over multiple continents and time zones, had become increasingly demanding. Her travel volume was so great that her youngest daughter knew the nanny better than her. With high organizational goals, Sara was willing to make tough choices and personal sacrifices to serve the company, up until she found herself on the precipice of complete burnout.

After an organizational change, the expectations to transform the organization's functional areas while at the same time cutting expenses and resources, managing a variety of workstreams, and transitioning team members to their new roles and responsibilities, became overwhelming. Sara, on the verge of total burnout, remained committed to her team's well-being and began to push back on their behalf. Her initial pushback fell on deaf ears, and her second attempt was interpreted as "negativity" and "lack of engagement." Sara ultimately made the difficult decision to resign, knowing she deserved to work for an organization that cared about her well-being and the well-being of her team.

The week prior to her resignation, Sara's boss was replaced without warning. She used the unexpected change as one final opportunity to stay at an organization she loved. Utilizing steps 1—acknowledge and empathize—and 2—state your perspective with clarity and respect—of GACM, she sat down with her new boss and said, "I understand you're in your first week of this position, and I know there is a great deal you're still learning. However, I feel it's important that I communicate my intention about my place here.

"I'd like to submit my letter of resignation next week. I recognized I was near complete burnout due to insurmountable expectations to transform the organization's functional areas while at the same time cutting expenses and resources, managing a variety of workstreams, and transitioning team members to their new roles and responsibilities.

"I shared my concerns with my boss, your predecessor, but was not supported. My values of family, leadership, and truth, which were once in line with the leader with whom I worked, had changed over the last few years. What are your thoughts on accommodating workload in order to retain great talent?"

Sara's new boss believed managers should have a vested interest in accommodating their employees and working out win/win situations. Aligned in their vision, Sara and her new boss developed a leadership wellness initiative focused on helping leaders reach their organizational goals while taking care of their physical and emotional health.

Now, it's time to climb up to level three of our building, the penthouse: the Graciously Assertive Lifestyle. It is here where you experience true transformation. This lifestyle allows you to live a life of gratitude, positivity, and growth. It is an extraordinary way to live and extremely rewarding.

I have helped thousands of women achieve a Graciously Assertive Lifestyle. They have transformed not only into phenomenal leaders but also into better human beings, better mothers, better wives, better daughters, better friends, and better community leaders. I'm here to help you do the same!

Spotlight: Dr. Daisy Gonzales

Below I share the powerful true testimony of a Latina woman who defied the odds that were stacked against her to become a successful leader in her community. She embodies what it means to be a Graciously Assertive Leader and continues to serve as an inspiration for every woman seeking to ascend the professional ladder. Be amazed as you read her heartwarming story.

Dr. Daisy Gonzales

Dr. Daisy Gonzales, Deputy Chancellor, California Community Colleges, is a student-centered leader. Her lifelong commitment to social justice, equity, and inclusion guides the empowerment of communities and encourages partnerships that enable economic mobility. Having served in higher education and statewide fiscal policy for more than twenty years, she currently serves as the second highest administrator for California's Community Colleges

Chancellor's Office, where she formulates policies distributing local assistance and capital outlay funds for 73 community college districts. She also designs programs to enhance student success and advocates for resources for learning environments for 1.9 million students.

Dr. Gonzales also worked tirelessly during the COVID-19 pandemic to secure historic levels of state funding and federal workforce investments, redesigning policies to make equitable access for all to higher education, and improving students outcomes. She continues to champion student success, college affordability, and equitable educational opportunities for all students by addressing students' basic needs, enhancing statewide technology investments, and supporting distance education quality.

She previously served as principal consultant for the California Assembly Appropriations Committee and Assembly Budget Committee and was named one of forty national Aspen Rising Presidential Fellows in 2019 and "Woman of the Year" by the Lieutenant Governor of California in 2021. Dr. Gonzales is a first-generation college student and a proud alumna of California's Community Colleges. She holds a BA in public policy and both an MA and a PhD in Sociology.

In Her Own Words

Dr. Yasmin: Tell me how your life story has propelled you to become the leader you are today.

Dr. Daisy: I grew up in the foster care system, but was born into a family of five children, all Mexican-American. My parents came to the U.S. as undocumented Mexicans and settled in the San Fernando Valley. At the age of two, I ended up in foster care, a fact I didn't realize until I was four. My earliest memory is being one of many children in tiny beds and adults taking care of us. At 13, I chose to stay in the foster care system and was ultimately required to testify against my own parents in court and tell of my abusive upbringing.

At the age of 17, I decided to emancipate myself from the foster care system on the advice of a social worker, who said that doing so would get me financial aid and allow me to go to college. This ended up not being true, and I ended up homeless. Fortunately, my chemistry teacher, Ms. Barker, offered for me to live with her until I graduated. Her condition? For me to go to college. And so, at 18, I flew off to Oakland, California to attend Mills College, an all-women school. It was there I found my voice.

Dr. Yasmin: How did you find your voice?

Dr. Daisy: There were 300 women my freshman year. Everyone lived in the same dorm, except for 10 commuters. Everyone knew one other. At Mills, I was one of only 14 women of color, all first-generation college students, on campus. We immediately felt we did not belong and became fast friends. Together, we did a summer program called the Summer Academic Workshop. We spent a month and a half taking math, English, and reading classes along with one sociology class to be better prepared for higher education.

I remember feeling I didn't belong, but at the same time having a great sense of responsibility for the other 13 women in the program with me. Along the way, I earned my voice as a straight-A student. One of the faculty members, Dr. Bruce Williams, often shared his personal story of being the son of slaves. He always said, "We have a great sense of responsibility as people of color, and we must make spaces to lift up others." That first summer, he pulled another student and me aside and congratulated us for our good grades. "But," he said firmly, "it is your job—your responsibility—to make sure your other colleagues, the other twelve, also get A's. That is what it means to work in sisterhood." I learned about sisterhood at Mills College.

I therefore learned the importance of speaking up for others, going as far as organizing a walkout when the college sought to increase tuition. Sitting in the president's office, I asked him, "What's your plan to make sure your students are not forced to give up their education?" At Mills, I learned I could use my voice for good. I learned I could open doors for others, so they could find and use their voice too.

Dr. Yasmin: How have you used your journey to shape the leader you are today?

Dr. Daisy: My journey taught me who I wanted to be and underscored who I did not want to be. Every day I was reminded in the foster care system that we were going to end up dead, pregnant, or in prison by 16. It is what we heard our entire lives. I knew that I did not want this for myself or my friends.

I was also deeply and positively impacted by the outliers, incredible human beings from all walks of life, like my bus driver in high school who would wait for me because the van that was supposed to transport me to an academic program was always late. It was a silent camaraderie between me and him, and we maintained a silent connection, every morning and afternoon, for three and a half years until he retired in my senior year. It was as though he knew I was going through a tough time and wanted to make sure I got to school.

Ms. Barker, my chemistry teacher, was another of these incredible human beings, as well as Dr. Williams, who was vulnerable enough to share his story and teach me how I could use my own story and gifts to help other people. He empowered me to know I was powerful and could make a difference.

My painful childhood, for which I am still undergoing a healing process, also taught me that even when things are bad, there are beautiful people who are generous and kind and who were influencing me to be my best self. I didn't see the beauty or generosity in my childhood home, but it didn't mean I couldn't become someone great. It is who I am as a leader, a combination of the bus driver who showed me that I was important enough to wait for, the teacher who lovingly opened up her home to me, and the sociology professor who told me, "You are powerful, and with great power comes a great responsibility: to help other people."

My painful childhood, for which I am still undergoing a healing process, also taught me that even when things are bad, there are beautiful people who are generous and kind.

Dr. Yasmin: What has been the most difficult time and greatest challenge you have faced in your life?

Dr. Daisy: I grew up with siblings, but after going to foster care, never had contact with them again. Though we all went through a lot as children, I was the one who knew from a very young age that our home was not safe, especially for a little girl, and that I needed to go to foster care. Being strong enough to testify in front of my own parents in a court was the hardest thing I did as a child. Reflecting on it now, it taught me to be a courageous leader.

As an adult, I feel blessed every day for the beautiful journey I've had as a human being and a leader. However, I still have triggers that remind me of my childhood trauma. For example, when overseeing my executive team and meeting with individuals, male or female, the door always has to be open. I recognize this comes from childhood, but it is now a part of who I am. Another thing that triggers me is that when I get an award, people often tell me, "Your parents must be so proud." I also find myself internally negotiating how much I want to share about my life with a complete stranger, but then realizing sometimes that being vulnerable can positively influence other people.

I've ultimately learned from my journey that there's great pain and trauma no matter how many years have passed. I've also learned I can self-heal, but it's a really lengthy process. I know I have surpassed expectations—against all odds, I didn't end up dead, pregnant, or in prison—but I'm still a work in progress. But although we all carry trauma, I have learned that it can also bond us too. As a foster youth, I had to adapt to so many strangers, to live in so many different environments, and to interact with so many diverse people. This experience strengthened my interpersonal skills and helped me as a leader.

I was also very observant as a child—because I often needed to be aware of my surroundings to determine if they were safe—and that skill has helped me know when I can be vulnerable, when I can share my story, and when my story is an opportunity to help me treat others with dignity and compassion.

Dr. Yasmin: You've taken your story and built your self-awareness, social awareness, and self-regulation. You use your story to build relationships, create safe spaces, and connect. How did you master these high-level emotional intelligence capabilities?

Dr. Daisy: It took time. I really had to learn and be self-aware. Education was the key to transforming my life, as were deep personal reflection and my role models. Every woman leader of color has her own equally impressive and unique story. I had to do the self-reflection, I had to be self-aware, and I had to understand and own my journey to get clear on my mission to transform California's public institutions and to serve Californians with dignity and compassion.

Every woman leader of color has her own equally impressive and unique story.

Dr. Yasmin: Do you believe your experience, through the process of self-awareness, has made you a better human being?

Dr. Daisy: Absolutely. When you grow up in foster care, people treat you with either kindness or cruelty. I can't tell you I was treated with dignity and compassion in every space, but I think the entire journey taught me what it is to be a human being. Those extraordinary humans, the outliers—the bus driver, the teacher, the professor—showed me who I could be if all of us were just better human beings. They gave me the hope and optimism I carry everywhere today. I am annoyingly optimistic—it doesn't matter how a day is going, I always strive to be positive. After all, there are worse things that could happen to me and that are happening to other people.

As leaders, we have to be aware that people are always going—or have gone—through something. We need to understand the bigger context. For me, it's a necessity. If we don't understand who we are as human beings and who we want to be, it becomes a liability. I need to know about the people I work beside if I want to transform the organizations in which I serve. It helps me motivate others.

For example, when I am hiring, in order to know if the candidate will work well with my team, I always ask, "If there was one word or phrase people could use to describe you, what would it be?" I always hire the same type of people, the people who tell me, "I'm a social justice warrior" or "I am a human rights advocate." There is a common theme, and it's doing bigger, better good. I need to know that you are seeking to do something bigger in the world, not the job title. If you want to join my team, I need to know you are in the habit of giving back.

I always need my team to understand everything on a global context because the work I do every day is transforming higher education. You can't transform higher education unless you're willing to see other people as human beings. It is social justice work, transformational work, work you can only do when you have a team who understand who they are and are willing to see others in a way to build effective strategies with compassion and dignity.

Dr. Yasmin: You have been identified as a Graciously Assertive Leader based on my 8 Pillars of Graciously Assertive Leadership. As a leader, which of the pillars do you identify most with and why?

Dr. Daisy: My journey began with self-awareness. If I don't know who I am, if I don't know I can truly be my authentic self, then I can't inspire others or help them be their true authentic selves. In the work space, helping others be their authentic selves means creating a safe working environment where everyone can present their best skills and talents and develop the best solutions. Even the way I start my executive staff meetings on Mondays begins with a quick check—your personal health, your mindset, your body, your family—before focusing on business. On Fridays, my team and I sit around together in a circle, discuss what we're grateful for, and give ourselves permission to enjoy the weekend. This, I know, is inspiring to others and helps us all with social awareness. I understand not all of my team members enjoy a team dynamic nor do they want to share everything about themselves. However, this practice, I have found, has allowed me to understand my team, cultivate trust, and inspire their passion for the journey of developing effective strategies.

My journey began with self-awareness. If I don't know who I am, if I don't know I can truly be my authentic self, then I can't inspire others or help them be their true authentic selves.

I credit social awareness with getting us through the global pandemic. I needed to know everything about my team—from who was sick at home to who was losing jobs in their families—because at the end of the day, I needed warriors to get higher education through a global pandemic. We had to tackle basic needs at scale, and I could not do it on my own.

When I really focused on my team, they were able to overcome all obstacles. It is truly a beautiful and powerful testimony.

Gratitude is another pillar with which I identify fully. Everything I do exemplifies gratitude. I am known for showing up at an event and saying, "I'm actually going to defer my time to my colleague." I don't call the people who work for me my staff; they are my colleagues. Or if I'm invited to speak, I may say, "This is actually about my team, so I brought three of my team members, and they are all powerful women of color." Suddenly, it becomes a panel because it was never about me.

Even the work I do today as the second-highest administrator for the largest public higher education system in the world is about the Graciously Assertive Leadership Pillars—being Graciously Assertive and a good communicator. Being a Graciously Assertive Communicator is key, even in the way I mentor. I also encourage my team to be more self-aware and strive to model gratitude. At the end of the day, I am the person who has to be held accountable. Even though I create the space and I mentor and model, it is in being a clear communicator that I have to deliver. I have to solve problems and empower others through the process.

I help people understand that we each have unique roles, authority, and responsibilities and that it is a foundation of empowerment and growth that makes us successful.

Dr. Yasmin: Self-Compassion is the pillar with which many powerful women struggle. Do you feel you have enough Self-Compassion?

Dr. Daisy: That's the one I struggle with most. As much as I care about treating other people with dignity and compassion,

I don't know if I have that same level of care for myself. For example, when I step off the stage, my husband will say, "Wow, that was incredible. That was a ten." I'm thinking, "Nah, that was a two."

I know I can be better at self-compassion, and now, I'm at a point in my life where I'm beginning to practice it more. Meditating and journaling has really helped me nurture my body and soul.

Dr. Yasmin: Many women in positions of power also struggle with the Healthy Boundaries Pillar. Do you?

Dr. Daisy: I was so good about healthy boundaries before the pandemic because I wanted to model it for my team. After 5:30 p.m., I would make sure the workday was ended, and every Thursday, I would not schedule any meetings. Then, with the pandemic, healthy boundaries went out the window. I'm trying to get it back now, starting with a new rule: no email replies after 6:00 p.m. on Fridays. If there is an emergency, we call each other.

Dr. Yasmin: My book *Graciously Assertive* defines a Graciously Assertive Leader as one who is direct and honest, yet kind and empathetic toward the feelings and needs of others. Do you feel you have always been a Graciously Assertive Leader?

Dr. Daisy: I feel like I've learned to be a Graciously Assertive Leader. It began when I was eleven years old, the youngest in my group home. All the foster kids were getting sick. They had rashes. It had been months since we had clean sheets. One of the kids said, "I've had enough. This is disgusting."

I answered, "I have a plan. Tomorrow we're going to refuse to go to school, so don't put on your clothes. Everyone take the sheets off the beds and we're just going to stand in front of the doors." Morning came, and we all stood in front of our doors with our bed sheets bundled up in a circle. The adults asked why were weren't ready for school.

We answered, "We want clean sheets." When they asked whose idea this was, all the kids pointed to me. We ended up negotiating with the adults and ultimately agreed that we would get ready for school, but only on the condition they take the sheets and put them in the washer.

Until then, I did not know I could use my voice for good. When I went to college, I learned more about using my voice for good when the question of raising tuition costs arose. In my sophomore year, when I felt alone because there were so few women of color, I created and launched a solidarity lounge that later became a cultural center at the campus. It is still there today.

These scenarios helped me become a Graciously Assertive Leader. I learned to empower others. We all have great ideas, but we have to speak up. The way I choose to lead now is all founded on Graciously Assertive Communication and leadership.

My prior job was in state service as a budget consultant for the state of California, managing $11.2 billion. When I got there, at age 24, I didn't realize that no one wanted the job. My first assignment was to cut health and human services by $750 million for the Department of Developmental Disabilities, the state agency that serves people with disabilities across the state of California. At the time, it was a sixty percent reduction.

I remember thinking, *I've got to figure out how to do this job and how to do it with dignity and compassion.* I sent a questionnaire to everyone in the organization who helped people with disabilities and got back twelve boxes of the same letter, stating, "Please don't cut us." It was not very helpful.

Next, I had to convene a budget stakeholder group and have them go around and discuss the cuts.

Even though I was new to the job, I did all the work to bring people together. Graciously, I said, "This is what I learned from all of you, but unfortunately, it is a really bad budget year. You will only be experiencing a $250 million reduction because together we have solved how we get $500 million in savings by securing additional resources from the federal government, additional reimbursements on this side." It really taught me about how I could use my voice for good and bring people together to do the work. I learned that it is all about being able to genuinely communicate yourself and say, "Here's what I've learned from you. Thank you for your best thinking, but this is a direction we're headed in and here's why."

Dr. Yasmin: Why do you think kindness is embedded in your leadership style?

Dr. Daisy: It goes back to the people who were so kind to me. It was my journey, and I went through it learning to give back and striving to do so. Kindness was cultivated in college, especially during the time I volunteered in a hospice care facility. It grew further when I read an article about foster kids being kept in cages. I knew I had to do something, so I ended up emailing everyone in the K–12 school district and the board of supervisors in Santa Barbara asking, "What are you going to do about this? You need to do something about it."

The school board members asked to meet with me for lunch. Sitting at a table together, one member suggested that I launch a summer program. I ended up creating a summer program that was operated by the foster kids, three of those who were kept in cages. It was in operation for five years and then was integrated into the local high school. The whole program I built was about empowering those students to know their story and to help them understand policy work. They did a summer research project in two groups. Group one worked on professional development for the group home staff. The other half examined why kids who aged out of the system often ended up in prison. From it all I learned that kindness leads to positive outcomes, and a lot of kindness is helping other people find their voice.

Dr. Yasmin: Why is being assertive, firm, and direct, in your leadership style important?

Dr. Daisy: I'm aware of what it looks like when I come into a room as a young Latina. If you don't know me, you make two assumptions: I don't know what I'm doing because I'm so young or the other people are the experts in the room. I love it when people make those assumptions because then I get to show them what a Graciously Assertive Leader I am. I can give you so many stories about when people undermined me and my team and we would simply walk out of the room together. Being assertive is about being clear about solutions because I believe in zero tolerance for inaction.

Dr. Yasmin: Do you believe your Graciously Assertive Leadership style has helped you to be a more effective communicator?

Dr. Daisy: Yes. I think a big component of being Graciously Assertive comes in the communication process. It's about validating others, hearing them out. If I've done my job right and I've built the right team, everyone can be their authentic selves and feel comfortable disagreeing with me. Those are opportunities for me to learn and for them to learn, because we all see things differently. To me, Graciously Assertive Leadership means no matter how gracious I am, I have to be held accountable, because that is what it means to be a leader.

I have to choose to be an effective communicator, as well. I'm gracious and understanding, and this allows my team members to be their authentic selves and give me their best solutions. And when I make the best decisions, I am able to empower others to do so as well.

Dr. Yasmin: In terms of organizational leadership, how do you deal with failure?

Dr. Daisy: Head-on; there is no other way. If you're doing real, authentic work to truly help people—if you're really seeking to transform institutions, organizations, structures—then you're going to make mistakes. I've learned, in leading during the global pandemic, that we made so many mistakes. I prefer to call them lessons, and we learned a lot from them. We must call out mistakes when they happen. It is the only way to move forward.

If you're doing real, authentic work to truly help people—if you're really seeking to transform institutions, organizations, structures—then you're going to make mistakes.

One of the biggest mistakes we make as leaders is not hiring the right people. I think a part of being kind and a Graciously Assertive Communicator is being able to tell people when they may not be in the right place.

Another important lesson is not moving too quickly. In empowering others, a leader has to understand the process is only as good as you are. If you fail to communicate, even though you empower, you will make mistakes. When you do, you have to boldly communicate, asking, "What could we have done differently?"

Dr. Yasmin: What happens when you have laid out your plans with your team and, for whatever reason, they haven't been able to deliver? How do you regroup and re-inspire people to double down on their efforts and move forward?

Dr. Daisy: I learned when my team is not performing, it's for one of three reasons. It may be a knowledge gap, which may mean I don't have the right team members in place, or we haven't quite acquired the right information. It could be burnout; they're tired. It could be morale. Whatever the cause, as the leader, I have to identify the reason so that I know how to handle it properly. If it's a knowledge gap, I want to understand what is missing and get the team member whatever is needed. If it's burnout, I need to ask them to take a break. If it's morale, I need to understand what is happening in the organization or what I may have done or not done and how it is impacting my team. Whatever the reason, I make the investment in my team to understand it. I work alongside them and help them find the solutions.

With morale and knowledge gaps, it's about creating spaces for learning. That's really what inspires people. I am an empathetic leader, and I want them to truly know who's being impacted so they can work through to the best solutions.

Dr. Yasmin: Who are the people you most admire when it comes to leadership? Why do you admire them? What influence have these people had on you?

Dr. Daisy: They're all women, and particularly women of color. Being a woman of color myself is a very unique experience and how I navigate the world. When people ask me, "What are the two identities you carry the most?" Number one is being a foster youth. Number two is being a woman. That's the order. When I think about all the women who have inspired me, who influence who I am, I remember the way they have navigated the world, what they have been able to accomplish, and how they are true to themselves. Their sense of spirit in creating solutions and inspiring others is very important to me. Finally, an important thing I have learned from all of these women is the way they communicate. They call people to action. They critique the status quo delicately and graciously.

Dr. Yasmin: Is there anything else you would like to share with the readers?

Dr. Daisy: I believe I've had an incredible life. I would have never imagined at age 11 that I would be where I am today. For many years, I didn't think I would live past 15, and even making it to 30 was always a dream. From being a K–12 teacher, from being a third-grade dual immersion teacher to the work I led at the statewide level for the budget committee, to the work I get to do now—which is an incredible honor as the first Latina in multiple roles for the largest system of public higher education—what I have learned is my journey was never about titles. If you're doing this type of work, if you're going to be a leader, you don't go off and pursue a career, or a sector, or a title; you go and pursue the goal which makes a difference.

I've also learned there's a difference between authority and real power. A title can give you authority and may get you through the door so people will listen, but real power is the ability to lead and have an entire team that invests themselves in your vision, building a pipeline for the future. Incredible things happen when you empower others.

When you build a healthy work environment, when you actually choose to see the human being, and when you are your true, authentic self, no matter how tired you may be one day, or how uninspired you may be another day, that pipeline you built will carry the work forward and make you proud. It is then you know you're a real leader.

Dr. Yasmin: Amen, sister. I love it. Beautiful.

Main Takeaways

Dr. Daisy Gonzales is a perfect example of a Graciously Assertive Leader. When a person embraces the Graciously Assertive Lifestyle, it becomes natural to communicate authentically and honestly and become a better human being. After all, everything about this transformation occurs at a deep spiritual level.

Graciously Assertive people naturally have a following because they are gracious, sensitive, and empathize with others and their situations. Their support and encouragement of their team members foster a community of opportunity and trust, and this community creates the perfect environment for leaders to actualize their vision.

When team members believe in their leader's vision, everyone becomes united. The vision becomes a shared vision, and the leader becomes its steward. This Graciously Assertive Leader is very clear about what success looks like for the team and holds those they lead accountable for doing their part. The leader is relentless about trying to keep the vision in constant focus, but tempers their determination with grace and kindness. A leader never tells a team member, "You failed." Instead, they say, "Look, I'm really depending on you. We have a vision of what we want to do. Last time, you didn't step up, but I have a great expectation for you to deliver next time. I believe in you. I know what you can do." This Graciously Assertive communication method is almost always effective because it encourages and guides the team member without putting him/her down.

Ultimately, a leader who speaks and leads with empathy and accountability will cultivate a successful team. They will inspire a shared vision and illustrate the power of mutual investment in which team members are inspired to reach the team's goals and are simultaneously taken care of by the leader.

CHAPTER THREE

THE ROLE OF MORALITY AND SPIRITUALITY IN GRACIOUSLY ASSERTIVE LEADERSHIP

Leading with morality and being Graciously Assertive go hand in hand. For the last 30 years, I have lived my life based on the eight foundational pillars of my Graciously Assertive philosophy and have found that morality plays a significant role in business. Think about it. Life and work aren't merely about what we do, how much we accomplish, or our successes; they are more about how we do what we do, how we achieve our goals, and how we define

As professionals, we are expected to conduct ourselves with the utmost integrity. We live in a world where moral lines are often blurred, particularly in business and leadership, so it is important to do what is right—both in the workplace and at home.

success. As professionals, we are expected to conduct ourselves with the utmost integrity. We live in a world where moral lines are often blurred, particularly in business and leadership, so it is important to do what is right—both in the workplace and at home.

Moral leadership requires us to lead with the values we hold dear and take the time to reflect, reconnect, rethink, and reimagine our lives.[6] It is exactly what the first pillar of Graciously Assertive Leadership—self-awareness—entails, as it involves being able to identify your values, align with them, and lead with them. Self-awareness not only helps leaders understand their strengths and weaknesses, but also helps them hold fast to their moral values and recognize their motives in life and work. A keen sense of self-awareness keeps leaders aligned to their values while allowing them to make sound decisions and grow their team to do the same.

Pillar 4, which is self-compassion, is connected to moral leadership, too, because it insists on the importance of caring for ourselves and—essentially—for others. Caring for others almost always involves doing what is right and upholding what is true and just. The pillar of self-regulation is also a huge factor in moral leadership. Controlling our emotions allows us to show kindness to others and encourages better communication, relationship growth, and a higher team engagement. When you regulate yourself, you are demonstrating the importance of conducting yourself in a right and proper way.

As moral leaders, it is crucial to foster open conversations. It is imperative that you engage dialogues, not one-way conversations in which the other party is ignored. After talking with you, do others say, "We had a great conversation"? If not, you need to take a moment and reevaluate how you communicate. As the eighth pillar of Graciously Assertive Leadership explains, you need to be both kind and assertive and hold space for others while in conversation, or else your relationships will suffer.

As moral leaders, it is crucial to foster open conversations. It is imperative that you engage dialogues, not one-way conversations in which the other party is ignored.

There may be nothing more moral than zero tolerance for judgment. Being a moral leader is doing the right thing, and we know that judging others is the opposite of doing the right thing. We can have our opinions, but judgment is different than opinion. Zero tolerance for judgment focuses on right behavior and the inherent goodness of humanity and helps leaders nurture a team that is collaborative, inclusive, and diverse.

Inclusivity and Moral Leadership

Inclusivity is morally right leadership. Inclusivity is complex. Moral leaders must embrace the complexity. In my experience working in the Diversity, Equity, and Inclusion (DEI) space, the depth and complexity behind the word "inclusivity" get lost when we think of it as an end goal versus a process. People are not, to use an analogy, different shapes to be put into a bucket, yet companies often position inclusion this way. The truth is that we don't know if we are being inclusive unless we open ourselves up for feedback on how people feel about being in this "bucket." Inclusion is, in essence, the feedback individuals provide us on the relationship we have. Based on the workplace we have created—the space where inclusion should occur—do those individuals feel seen, valued, and respected?

If we think about inclusion as a phenomenon, then inclusivity is undeniably more of a process and, more specifically, a relational one. Our ability to see others in their diversity and respect their worldviews must be strong. We must be able to hear feedback that lets us know what the company has done to mold its real climate and culture—is it vibrant or does it cause harm? Most organizations do not want raw diversity, equity, and inclusion-oriented feedback because too many people still see DEI not as "real work" or rather as barriers to the work. Yet, people are the center of any business, regardless of how many processes we automate. It is nonnegotiable—companies must become more inclusive or risk employee morale and engagement and, then, their bottom line.

If I look at the "ingredients" I use in the process of fostering inclusion, I see some of them in many companies and organizations. Naturally, each entity has different degrees of inclusion, but I continually notice a weak awareness of how deep the relational involvement must be in order to create workplaces that are inclusive to all who are employed there. I say weak not as a way to say ignorant but as a way to highlight naivety.

Yes, companies and organizations want to acknowledge the unique backgrounds and experiences of their employees. They know there is value in diversity. But, what happens when individuals feel unseen because of the trauma and harm they have experienced from discrimination in their personal lives or from being a member of a historically discriminated-against community? Many managers are not ready to respond to the symptoms of past harmful traumas and the resulting distrust developed by employees as a result. Whether we like it or not, if we want diversity, then we have to be ready to respond and act because, as previously stated, diversity is not a label; it is a lived experience.

In *Social, Cultural, and Other Diversity Issues in the Traumatic Stress Field*, the National Institutes of Health reported that culture, ethnicity, gender, sexual orientation, and disability are potential sources of resilience, but they also may lead to chronic stressors such as social stigma, discrimination, and oppression, which can increase psychological trauma and PTSD.[7]

Given that ethnocultural, natural, gender, age, and disability characteristics are crucial in also defining identity, it is no surprise that trauma, whether at work, in life, or as part of a community, adversely impacts identity. When identity is used to stigmatize, discriminate, or present a socioeconomic disadvantage, then traumatic stressors compound the effects, but when these vulnerabilities are addressed responsibly in the workplace, social justice can prevail.[8]

Given that ethnocultural, natural, gender, age, and disability characteristics are crucial in also defining identity, it is no surprise that trauma, whether at work, in life, or as part of a community, adversely impacts identity.

Consider these scenarios. What happens when leaders are respectful and nonjudgmental—how do employees feel? What happens when a leader compassionately holds space to have an employee focus on what's within their control—how do employees feel? Now, what happens when the two are combined? Among the most powerful combinations an individual can have in the workplace is 1) engaging with a colleague who is compassionate, respectful, and nonjudgmental, 2) a colleague who can see them holistically and guide them on reasonable next steps, and 3) practicing these next-step commitments in an organization which has been intentional in creating a culture where workplace trauma is managed like the organizational risk it is.

Too often, organizations usher in representation in a numerical way—tabulating identities and monitoring their demographic composition. Far less often is there a nuanced strategy to address the culture and climate so the organization is felt as inclusive. In doing so, promotions are handled equitably, discrimination is promptly addressed, toxic colleagues are not tolerated, and people are not tokenized.

If an employee with an underrepresented identity is invited to the table and does not feel a sense of belonging, inclusion is not working in the organization, and we as leaders are not acting morally. An individual can easily encounter conversations, comments, behaviors (and, to be more specific, microaggressions, harassment, retaliation, bullying, and more) when the space's dominant cultural norms are interculturally immature or focused on the workplace cultural norms of a specific generation (e.g., Boomers, Gen X, Millennials, Gen Z). Scenarios such as these are not ever good for business.

If an employee with an underrepresented identity is invited to the table and does not feel a sense of belonging, inclusion is not working in the organization, and we as leaders are not acting morally.

Another way to consider inclusivity as a process is understanding that organizations must practice critical mirror work and learn their own organizational struggles. It is an examination of why they may be resistant, fearful, or hesitant to be honest with themselves on how much work they will do to meet people in their diversity. It is being a better person and seeking the inherent goodness in others. For example, companies are hesitant to chip away at harmful ideologies (e.g., stereotypical thinking, insensitive jokes) because doers of these behaviors, who often have a lot of organizational clout, feel "it's not a big deal" or "people are just too sensitive." Let's ask ourselves, *Would you want to work with coworkers who dehumanize you in a space where your company does nothing about it?*

Too often a person who has challenges in the workplace is labeled as emotionally dysregulated. Maybe the individual brings up issues that have "nothing to do" with the work context. An individual may be facing some huge challenge or require some deep healing, but we question ourselves: *What is it about this workplace environment that is so triggering? Why hasn't this individual had access to workplace conversations that will help them navigate with success?* Both of these examples highlight that the inclusion equation requires real relational efforts on behalf of the organization to honor the truest depth of the diversity brought by its team members.

It is exactly what I mean by saying, "Inclusion work can be complex, but it is right." When personnel incidents occur, it is incredibly difficult to pinpoint the issue which activated the reaction/response. Was it the words spoken at a meeting, or the memory triggered and linked to a person's social identity? Was it the double whammy of both? It is the reason leaders—whether HR professional or DEI expert—must strategically develop initiatives to create the felt experience of inclusion. When we bring people of diverse backgrounds into a workplace, there is a responsibility for the organization to develop the climate and experiences. Activities such as grievance processes, morale activities, and inclusive talent development all work to create a space where inclusion occurs for all. At large, inclusivity is an area of expertise that blends the psychology of trauma and wellbeing and the canon of equity, diversity, and inclusion strategies. Inclusivity is morally right. It is zero tolerance for judgment. It is complex, yet moral leaders embrace the complexity.

Furthermore, we cannot be moral leaders without healthy boundaries. We have to be able to say no to people who are not doing the right thing. We have to set our boundaries and be firm in them.

Moral leadership, broken down simply, means doing the right thing, listening to people, and making them feel safe, no matter what.

Moral leadership, broken down simply, means doing the right thing, listening to people, and making them feel safe, no matter what.

The 8 Pillars of Graciously Assertive Leadership fall right in line with being a moral leader, as they help demonstrate who you are, disclose your values, determine how you make decisions and lead, as well as how you communicate and interact with others. By embracing the 8 fundamental Pillars of Graciously Assertive Leadership and the moral authority suggested by them, we can bring out the best in ourselves and our teams and grow a new generation of confident, moral leaders. To quote Dov Seidman, "without hope, there is no strategy. Moral leaders purvey hope, and they inspire hope in others by really helping them see possibility, helping them embrace the commonality in the other, so that we can do things together."[9]

Spirituality and Graciously Assertive Leadership

Graciously Assertive Leadership also has a strong spiritual component. Honestly, everything about my approach is spiritual.

Let me explain. I am not religious, but I am extremely spiritual, and I embrace spirituality in ways I will never be able to comprehend. My faith in a power greater than myself is so strong that it drives and sustains me and has imbued my life with meaning. After all, to grow as a leader means to evolve as a human being, to change, to become.

There are nine signs indicating someone is experiencing a spiritual transformation:

- the collapse of old negative habits,
- the opening of new doors,
- letting go of negativity,
- the release of self-perception,
- the exit of negative influences,
- the rise of new insights into reality,
- purging and detoxification,
- greater security and trust, and
- enhanced levels of love and compassion.[10]

First in spiritual transformation is allowing our old ways to disintegrate, so new doorways open. As old habits depart, new areas of life open up, and profound life insights are gained. Next comes the challenge of energetic purging and detoxification, which rids the self of negative actions and energies which can disrupt every area of life. As these are released, individuals garner more inner security, develop greater trust, and grow in their capacity for love and compassion.

Another sign of spiritual transformation is letting go and surrendering. When we finally let go and just become who we were meant to be, we can evolve. As successful women, we often try to control everything. We see control as the reason for success. We try to control our children, our partners, our lives, every single thing, and it inevitably becomes overwhelming. We have to allow ourselves to be, not just to do.

Going through the spiritual transformation of our program allows women to let go and surrender because they are encouraged to believe in the greatness within themselves and embrace change. Self-identity slackens as women begin to see themselves in new ways.

In doing so, we as women and leaders can capture the genuine essence of ourselves as better leaders and better humans. We are inspired because our spiritual transformation aligns so perfectly with the Graciously Assertive Lifestyle.

As we go forward on this journey together, I'll share the stories of transformation which align with each of these nine signs. The women who have experienced it describe their old ways—how they previously viewed the world and themselves—as disintegrating. As they undergo this spiritual transformation, new opportunities avail themselves. As a result, the women become more gracious. They're no longer angry.

As women have embraced the spiritual transformation and engaged with their newly transformed selves, some people in their lives leave. After their departure, the women identified those with whom they used to engage as having had a certain negative energy. Now, these women want to perpetuate positivity and hope, experience the healing and the shedding of shame, and start moving away from those negative people.

My students also gain profound insights into the nature of reality. They begin to ask spiritual questions even if they were never spiritual before. The most common questions include:

- What is my greater purpose in life?
- How do I want to impact the world?
- How do I become a better human being?
- What will my legacy be?

These questions and more start to figure in their lives even though they never had before. They allow women to recognize that they could make the world better.

As my students experience spiritual transformation, they go through energetic purging and detoxification as part of the process.[11] As women begin to refuse to allow negative energy in their lives, they find the power within themselves to leave the jobs and personal relationships that are toxic to them. It is a large part of what women go through in my program as they learn to embrace both graciousness and assertiveness.

As they begin to embrace this transformation, women encounter greater security and trust in their lives. We see it frequently in their stories. They begin to believe in themselves, embrace their true purpose, and:

- Let go,
- Trust life,
- And see everything as a gift.

They trust that no matter what happens to them, they'll be able to find the gift in it. It is beautiful. It is spiritual.

The final aspect of spiritual transformation in Graciously Assertive Living is deepening love and compassion every day. Everything I do, everything I say, everything I teach, and everything I am are about love and compassion.

In Her Own Words

Reese

Dr. Davidds' leadership program helped me go through a spiritual and neural transformation that changed how I perceive and respond to the people, environments, and the world around me. It gave me the confidence to rearrange each of those factors in correlation with my core values with uncompromising grace.

This transformation for me was both sudden and intentional. I started by taking inventory of the people within my inner circle and sphere of influence. Because the program put me in such a positive spiritual mindset, it was all the more apparent when other people's negative energy affected my own. I was able to feel the contrast between my energy when I was with my leadership program sisters and how I felt around others outside the program. Relationships with people who were a complete contradiction to how I wanted to feel became obvious to me. I began to observe whether conversations were negative or positive and if interactions left me feeling drained or energized. I tried to help those of my friends and colleagues with negative energy see the brighter outlook on their situations, but when it became clear they had no desire to be freed from the muck and mire of their own negative thoughts, I had to stop engaging them. This allowed me to preserve my inner peace and positivity.

As I observed this shift in energy, I was able to sense the state of peace certain environments either nurtured or destroyed. Since I spent most of my time at work both during and after the leadership program, I began to see how interacting with certain team members had become destructive to my inner peace and detracted from my core values of respect and integrity. Therefore, I knew when the return on investment of staying where I was had diminished, and I had no problem walking away and stepping into a new role. Until that role came, I had to dig deep into my spirituality to weather the storm and not lose hope that better days were coming, which can sometimes be the hardest part of transformation.

With so much going on in the world around us, it is difficult not to be influenced and distracted from our values and priorities (life's big rocks). This rang true for me during the pandemic in 2021, when I was in the midst of working a job I didn't love, homeschooling two young sons under lockdown, and volunteering as a youth advocate for a nonprofit, which often felt like a thankless job. Soon, I broke out in a rash that scarred over a third of my body and was diagnosed with an auto-immune disorder, lichen planus, which caused my body's immune system to attack my healthy skin cells. Studies have linked this disorder to stress, and so I realized that I needed to shift my mind back toward my values, goals, and priorities, and regulate my stress. Once I did this, the symptoms of the condition began to subside. I had gotten so far away from spiritual centeredness that my body captured my attention by outwardly projecting the toxicity I was harboring inside. In this situation, I was reminded of the teachings from the program, and I recommitted to my core values, goals, and life mission to be a beacon of hope. I applied to business school, left my position as vice president, and thrust my energy into being an academic ambassador for my school, where I get to coach, develop, and uplift prospective and current students.

The Graciously Assertive Model versus Other Leadership Approaches

I'm often asked, "How is your model, the Graciously Assertive model, different from other leadership models?" I think morality and spirituality, as well as graciousness and assertiveness, make my model unique and effective. There are many different leadership approaches, each different, but I have never found one like mine. After all, its basis is kindness, love, compassion, and gratitude—qualities that rarely take precedence in leadership business models. It insists that in order to be a better leader, one must first become a better human, and vice versa.

When I began my programs, I started interviewing thousands of women and asking them about how they were living their lives after the program and the subsequent transformation. I reviewed all the transcripts, highlighting the similarities, noting the patterns, and determining what they had accomplished by leading and living in gracious ways. It helped me to discern the concepts that allowed them to flourish with self-awareness, leading and living through their values, social awareness, self-regulation, and emotional intelligence.

The process of developing my Graciously Assertive model was, in itself, a spiritual experience.

Let me share one story. No matter how evolved we are, we all still have a long way to go. During the COVID-19 pandemic, I hired a leadership consultant to help me develop a more robust framework for my Leadership Development Institute. As we began, she asked me all sorts of questions. I had all this homework prepared in order to answer her.

She interviewed me, recorded each interview, jotted down notes. I talked about how important it is for people to be kind, to be empathetic, to be Graciously Assertive. For a point of reference, I went on and on about the importance of being empathetic to another person's story. I was very passionate about explaining and justifying my point, when she asked me a question that gave me pause: "Why should anybody care what you're saying?"

I felt a little strange. *Why shouldn't everybody care?* I wondered. Without thinking, I answered, "Because it's about humanity. Everything I'm talking about is about being the best human being you can be. In this world, if we all focus on being the best version of ourselves, then this world will be a better place. We simply can't be better if we're not leading by example.

The best gift, the greatest gift, the most loving gift we can contribute to the world, is for us to continuously become the best version of ourselves, mind, body, and soul. When we do, we will heal. We will become better to people. We will treat others better. We will be more ethical.

The best gift, the greatest gift, the most loving gift we can contribute to the world, is for us to continuously become the best version of ourselves, mind, body, and soul.

The better we show up for ourselves, the less we hurt others, and the better the world will be as a result. After all, hurt people hurt other people in turn. When we have healed, we will still hurt people, but now we will become more aware and strive to release our pain in other ways and not be toxic to others.

My leadership consultant then said, "You know, you didn't mention you've been focusing your business for the last twenty years on empowering and developing women. Everything you shared was about humanity."

"What do you mean?" I asked.

"It's all about humanity," she said. "What you've been talking about is your passion."

Wait a minute. Does she mean I'm supposed to empower and develop humanity? I thought. This all sounded crazy to me.

All my life I had been empowering and developing women. I'd been very successful, having gone from empowering and developing just Latinas to women of other cultures, to all women.

I didn't say it aloud, but in mind, I was thinking, *I can't help all of humanity, could I?* I didn't feel worthy; I didn't feel I had the capacity. *Who the heck am I?* I wondered. I was too small. I was convinced that I did not have what it takes to help people, regardless of gender.

Finally, I declared, "No, that's way too much. I don't even want to go there. I don't want to talk about it." It was just so overwhelming in that moment.

Then, the consultant told me something that completely changed my life, and it still gives me chills when I think about it. She spoke plainly: "You have some homework for tonight. There is one question that I want you to think about. I want you to ask yourself how long it is going to take for your mind to catch up to your soul."

"What are you talking about?" I asked, perplexed.

She smiled. "Your soul is already there. It thinks and speaks about humanity, leadership, global leadership, world leaders minimizing and eliminating ego. Yet, your mind is holding you back. Your mind is stuck on women. Women are great, but you're beyond that now, and you are your greatest limitation. Your mind is your greatest limitation because your soul is already there."

Immediately, I began to cry. I had never thought that I could help all people. The concept was just too grand. I put it in the back of my mind since I knew I wasn't ready to face or embrace it.

Back then, I didn't even realize I—and no other external force—had become the greatest limitation to myself. At the time, it was too overwhelming to even consider that I had the capacity to ignite and talk about humanity and global leadership and how we need to bring humanity and true moral leadership together.

Today, I know moral leadership is what is needed throughout the world. Mayhem—in the form of war, racism, sexism—is everywhere. People take sides, and it becomes ugly. I truly believe that people are inherently good, but unfortunately there are few moral leaders who are willing and courageous enough to lead us past our differences and to guide us to be better humans. If we strive, we can become the next Jacinda Arderns, Michelle Obamas, Martin Luther King Jrs., Gandhis, and Nelson Mandelas of the world.

If we strive, we can become the next Jacinda Arderns, Michelle Obamas, Martin Luther King Jrs., Gandhis, and Nelson Mandelas of the world.

This conversation with my leadership consultant happened nearly three years ago. Since then, I realized that I needed more. I needed to have conversations about humanity, about global leadership, about moral leadership. But with whom? I realized that I needed to put myself in an academic environment where I could have them.

I have my doctorate, and I have always wanted to get an executive MBA, so I realized that it was time to up my game and step into a world of intellectual stimulation. Everything aligned, and it seemed to be the proper time. I applied and was accepted to one of the most prestigious executive MBA programs in the country. Everyone was phenomenal, but soon I realized that folks were having the same conversations I was having ten years ago in my Institute classroom.

I had to ask my professors: "Where are the conversations about moral leadership, global leadership, humanity, being better humans to be better leaders?" No one had an answer. It seems that they didn't really know what I meant. My concerns about how predetermined rights and wrongs factored into leadership and the path to greater good were outside the realm of current conversations, or at least not part of the ones I was hearing.

The conversations in my classes were intriguing, but they were very basic. They were about moving up in an organization, getting a better position, and teamwork. All great, all important, but they weren't what I was seeking. I yearned for depth, and I was desperately seeking soulful conversations about how to elevate our global leadership conversations to speaking the truth. Unless our world and organizational leaders begin to heal their traumas, I believed, they will continue to hurt people and deny the world their full potential.

I went into the Executive MBA program to get my cup filled, but instead I felt empty. There was nothing wrong with what was happening in these classrooms, but I was in a different place.

My coach instantly set me straight, and it was mind-blowing. "You're not getting anything out of this experience right now, yet you are compelled to stick with it. You're exhausted. You're putting work into it, but it's not bringing you any value for what you want to do." Next she asked, "If this was the case with one of your students, what would you tell her?"

I answered truthfully. "I would tell her to exit immediately, even though money, time, and energy had already been invested."

I realized I had so many huge projects coming my way, and I was going to have to make a choice: school or the growth of my company. I simply could not do both. Within a half hour of that conversation with my coach, I withdrew from the program. It was a relief to be able to do what was right for me.

However, it had not been a waste. It demonstrated for me that I should never be fearful of shifting pathways if I was not growing or evolving. The program was there to show me I didn't need validation; I already had validation. It lit a fire under me: If the conversations I was desperately searching for weren't being had, I needed to create them.

The meeting with my coach ultimately opened my eyes to see that I had the willpower and ability to make a change. I had to let go and surrender, so my identity could shift, and I could see myself as a thought leader.

CHAPTER FOUR

DEVELOPING AS A GRACIOUSLY ASSERTIVE COMMUNICATOR

Becoming a Graciously Assertive Communicator requires following a simple four-step model. We'll begin our development with an overview of the model, then dive into examples of how to use it. The model itself is about acknowledging and empathizing. It begins by listening in earnest to the other person's perspective actively, then empathizing with and acknowledging their feelings and concerns. The next step encourages you to state your perspective with clarity and respect. Step one therefore requires graciousness, and step two requires assertiveness.

Step three consists of finding common ground with the person and identifying shared goals. The final step is determining a collaborative solution. Steps three and four combine graciousness and assertiveness, as this will help you get the message across and reach a beneficial and collaborative solution.

The Components of Being a Graciously Assertive Communicator

We've covered the models steps in brief, so now let's take a deeper look at the communication model of a Graciously Assertive Communicator. It is a solid communication model for women and is based in self-advocacy. The model works for men as well. While most communication models can be used to self-advocate, our goal here is to self-advocate while communicating with people in ways that help people feel seen, heard, and included. It is beneficial for everyone in the conversation and creates win-win scenarios.

Showing empathy, proposing solutions, and being able to collaborate are all crucial human needs and therefore should be integral in all sophisticated communication models. Being heard, empathizing, and helping others feel heard and understood allow people to self-advocate and hold space for others, as well as for themselves.

Showing empathy, proposing solutions, and being able to collaborate are all crucial human needs and therefore should be integral in all sophisticated communication models.

Effective communication models must embrace humanity and demonstrate how human beings should interact. The following is the four-step communication model that Graciously Assertive Communicators use to practice and hone their skills:

1. **Acknowledge and Empathize:** Begin by genuinely listening to the other person's perspective. Show empathy by acknowledging their feelings and concerns.

2. **State Your Perspective with Clarity and Respect:** Express your viewpoint using "I" statements to clearly communicate your thoughts, needs, and/or boundaries. Maintain a respectful tone and avoid blaming or judging.
3. **Find Common Ground and Shared Goals:** Identify areas of agreement or mutual interests between your perspective and the other person's. Emphasize the shared goals you both have in order to build rapport.
4. **Collaboratively Propose Solutions:** Present potential solutions that consider both parties' concerns and align with shared goals. Invite their input and ideas, fostering a sense of collaboration and partnership.

By following our communication model, a Graciously Assertive Communicator can effectively navigate challenging conversations, promote open dialogue, and build strong relationships while asserting their needs and establishing boundaries.

For example, one of my students, Julia, had the opportunity to demonstrate these four steps in a very high-stakes jury deliberation.

It was a powerful experience for her. Never did she think participating in jury duty would allow her to effectively use the Graciously Assertive Communication Model in such a compelling way. The lessons learned from this experience show the power of Graciously Assertive Communication and how it overlaps in all aspects of life.

The four steps do not always have to happen sequentially, but they do all have to happen to reach the best solution. In fact, you will revisit many of the steps over and over to reach your goal. Staying focused on these four steps and revisiting every step when needed will guide you to your desired outcome.

The court case in itself was a painful one, as it involved a police shooting of an unarmed Latino man. A police officer shot the man six times, killing him.

Julia was sitting in the jury deliberation room with seven men. She was the only woman in the jury. They had been in the courtroom for six days, listening to all the expert witnesses, reviewing photos of the scene and watching re-enactments of what the prosecution argued had happened the evening of the killing. As jury rules go, jurors are not allowed to talk about the case until the very last day, when they step into the deliberation room to make a final decision on their findings. The prosecution's argument was the unarmed man was shot six times; the two he took in the back were the ones that killed him. The defense argued the shots occurred when the unarmed man rushed the police officer; thus, the officer acted in self-defense. According to the defense, it was when the man turned slightly away that the shots hit him in the back.

Julia had spent the last six days of jury duty building connections with each of the seven jurors to ensure they would listen to her perspective from a place of credibility and respect. The situation could be likened to a corporate boardroom with corporate board members making important decisions. Obviously, there were differences, but the importance of Graciously Assertive communication was key and also had high financial implications.

Julia felt the evidence presented clearly proved negligence by the officer who shot the unarmed man. As she sat in the jury deliberation room, she proposed a temperature check to see where each juror stood before they began deliberation. They all agreed. She began by calling on Juror #1, a white man in his sixties, who was a retired computer consultant. He had garnered a significant amount of respect from the group, mostly because of his strong presence and quiet demeanor. He didn't say much, yet when he spoke, all the men listened. Therefore, getting him on her side was important because his vote and voice held influence. This strategy—borrowed power—is common in business and politics. It holds that the person with the most power in the room—if they align in values, thoughts, and/or ideas—can be useful to your cause, if needed. To Julia's relief, Juror #1 was leaning toward guilty. However, to her shock, the rest voted not guilty or explained that they were not fully sure yet.

This strategy–borrowed power–is common in business and politics. It holds that the person with the most power in the room–if they align in values, thoughts, and/or ideas–can be useful to your cause, if needed.

She couldn't understand how so many of the jurors saw things so differently than she did, even when they all were presented with the same information. Julia had committed her professional career to victim advocacy, specifically advocating for survivors of domestic violence. She was sensitive to violence toward other human beings, so she knew she would have to manage her emotions during this process. She was full of emotions, but knew she needed to stay calm and fully understand each juror's perspective and try to empathize with them. She knew she needed to do something to move out of her emotions and into a strategic process of communication. She chose to practice the four steps of Graciously Assertive Communication and take control of the situation.

Scenarios like this show up every day in business conference rooms, boardrooms, offices, and within teams. It is up to you to identify what you need to do to be able to persuade, get buy-in, influence, negotiate, or whatever you want to call it to change people's minds.

Julia knew that as emotionally charged as she was, she would have to follow the four steps as needed and probably revisit a few of them.

Step one of the Graciously Assertive Communication Model is to "acknowledge and empathize by actively listening." She knew she could not move on to step two—stating her viewpoints, using "I" to clearly communicate her thoughts—until each of the six men felt heard and understood by her. It was also crucial to not use an accusatory tone. She had to get out of her own ego and focus on their thought process if she wanted them to extend the same courtesy to her. Julia had to keep the communication channels open in order for them to be open to listening to her.

Not only did she need to listen to the other jurors empathetically, but she needed to manage her emotions in the process. Scenarios like these are common in everyday life and business. We may not agree with what's on the table, but we cannot allow our emotions to take over. We have to understand and respect why the other side feels the way they feel or believes what they believe—especially if we want to change their mind. We cannot influence or change their mind in any way unless we understand them.

We have to understand and respect why the other side feels the way they feel or believes what they believe—especially if we want to change their mind. We cannot influence or change their mind in any way unless we understand them.

It was a tall order for Julia, but she knew it had to be done, and with GACM in hand, she was ready. She started with Juror #2. "Help me understand," she began, "why you believe he is not guilty?"

He responded, "As a man, we are taught to protect others at whatever cost necessary. I feel I probably would've done the same thing if I was put in that officer's position. He acted like any man would to protect whatever he needed to protect."

Julia, frustrated by his lack of empathy for the unarmed man who was shot, reminded herself that it was important for her to listen, acknowledge, and empathize. She took a deep breath, pulling herself out of her judgment mindset and surrendering herself to being a witness to his vulnerability, in order to hold space for him. She needed him to feel safe enough to share how he felt. She offered the same courtesy to each of the other jurors. Adhering to the principles of the Graciously Assertive Communication Model, she listened, acknowledged, and empathized for as long as was needed. After all, her hope was that doing so would ensure each juror felt that his feelings and concerns were heard.

She then moved to vocalizing her empathy with the jurors. She said, "Gentleman, I completely understand your need to protect others. As men in society, you are taught—and expected—to do whatever it takes to protect others. Not only do I hear each one of you, but I honor and thank each of you for that." Julia looked at each juror in the eyes as she spoke these words. (Note: Do not ever try to fake your acknowledgment and validation of others; it needs to be genuine, or it will backfire.)

Once she felt she had completed step one and each juror felt understood and listened to, Julia was ready to move to step two: state your perspective with clarity and respect.

"Gentlemen," she continued, "I highly respect each and every one of your perspectives. Now, I'd like to share with you some information for you to take into consideration." Julia then proceeded to state her points and clearly communicate her thoughts. She argued that this case had started with an emergency 5150 call—a phone call that alerts law enforcement that a person is experiencing mental distress. Officers in California are trained for these types of calls, and therefore the police officer should have known to use his taser or pepper spray. She further reinforced that the officer had advance notice that the victim was in the midst of a mental health crisis.

Julia continued to explain that officers must shoot only to stop a threat of bodily harm. The officer made a conscious choice to use his gun, instead of employing his 5150 training, which called to use his taser gun or pepper spray. The men listened intently to her words. Even though she disagreed with them, they gave her the same respect she had shown them earlier.

Once Julia felt they were open and really listening to her, she realized it was time to move to the third step of GACM: find common ground. She asked them, "How many of you are parents?" Four raised their hands, so she went a step further.

"How many of you have boys?" she asked.

The same four raised their hands, so Julia posed another question: "What if the man with the mental health illness was your son? What if your son was suffering from a schizophrenic episode or was having a mental breakdown? Would you want a police officer to shoot to kill or would you prefer he use a taser, pepper spray, or wait for backup? For those of you who don't have children, what if the victim was your brother? Your father?"

Julia stayed quiet for a few moments, allowing the jurors to soak in everything she said. She could tell it hit home for the men when she spoke about their loved ones. As many learn throughout their life and career, if you want someone to truly understand your perspective, personalize it. Find out what the person you're attempting to influence values and reframe the situation, so they can see it in a way they have never seen before. When Julia reframed the situation in a way that became personal, everything changed for the jurors. At first, they had empathized with the police officer as a protector, but now they were beginning to empathize with the victim as fathers and family members themselves.

Julia took a temperature check to see what her fellow jurors were thinking in order to gauge if she could move to the second part of step three: identify shared goals. At this, Juror #1 said: "Well, the officer didn't have to shoot six times. He could have used his 5150 mental health issue training."

Everyone in the room immediately began buzzing with enthusiasm and agreed. Julia was floored. Hadn't she just said the same thing? She was ultimately experiencing what every professional woman experiences at some time or another, whether in a corporate, academic, or political arena. It is known as "hepeating," when a woman proposes an idea, which is dismissed or ignored, before a male presents the same idea, which is then acknowledged or praised. She had to do something.

"Thank you," Julia told Juror #1 politely, "for agreeing with my point that the police officer did not have to shoot six times. I'm happy our thoughts align." Here, Julia had found common ground, so she continued, "Gentlemen, if the officer's job is to protect and serve humanity, and his vow as an officer is to avoid deadly force at all costs, can we agree this type of behavior is reckless?"

Julia was relieved to hear that all the men agreed with her. Now, it was time to determine a shared goal. She asked,

"Can we agree our goal is to do justice for the victim and his family?" Though it took hours, the Graciously Assertive Communication Model came through in a real-life, high-stakes scenario. Julia was able to help effect real change by being firm yet kind and respectful. Never once did she compromise her beliefs nor make another juror feel unheard or dismissed. The Graciously Assertive Communication Model can yield similar results in any situation in life, in business or in academia, as long as you take the time to follow the steps and repeat as needed.

Self-Advocacy in Graciously Assertive Communication

Let's backtrack a minute. Earlier I made a point about why men in power rarely take strong and fast action to put more women in positions of power when research shows companies are more profitable if they do. Why is this? I'll tell you: everything comes down to power.

In the over-30 discussions I've had with men in extremely powerful positions, I have found that the conclusion is always the same. There are only so many positions of power, held mostly by men, and these positions of power do not come often, usually becoming available only when a successor for each position of power has been identified (by either the person holding the position or other men in positions of power) and long before the position is open. Human nature is to move toward and attract people who are like you, those with whom you are most comfortable. Therefore, men, for the most part, select successors with whom they feel most comfortable or those who have been most loyal to them.

Furthermore, one of many other reasons women are often overlooked when it comes to ascending the corporate ladder is their inability to self-advocate. So, what is self-advocacy? Self-advocacy is understanding and recognizing one's rights, responsibilities, and values and having the confidence to stand up for oneself, especially in situations where one's well-being or rights might be compromised. Being "Graciously Assertive" in self-advocacy melds two essential qualities: graciousness and assertiveness.

Self-advocacy is understanding and recognizing one's rights, responsibilities, and values and having the confidence to stand up for oneself, especially in situations where one's well-being or rights might be compromised.

Graciousness involves approaching situations with kindness, tact, and consideration. Being gracious means you're respectful in your interactions, even when you are standing up for your rights or expressing your needs. It's about maintaining dignity and showing appreciation, even in challenging conversations.

Assertiveness is the ability to express one's feelings, beliefs, opinions, and needs directly, openly, and honestly, all while respecting the rights of others. Being assertive means you value yourself, stand up for your rights without being aggressive, and effectively communicate your needs and concerns.

When combined, being "Graciously Assertive" in self-advocacy means:

1. You clearly and confidently communicate your needs and rights.
2. You respect the viewpoints and rights of others, ensuring a balanced dialogue.

3. You're proactive in seeking understanding and solutions, rather than being passive or aggressive.
4. You remain polite and considerate, avoiding blame or judgment, even when facing resistance or challenges.

Therefore, the question is: How do we, as women, advocate for ourselves in the workplace as Julia was able to do in the jury deliberation room? The answer is simpler than you think. Let's consider this scenario. You're working on a team project and feel your ideas are consistently overlooked during team meetings. How can you apply the Graciously Assertive Communication Model to self-advocate for acknowledgment?

1. **Acknowledge and Empathize**
   Approach: "Hey John, I've noticed that during our last few meetings, there's been a lot of enthusiasm around certain ideas. I really appreciate the energy everyone's bringing to the table."
   Why This Works: By acknowledging the group's enthusiasm, you show you value and recognize their input. This makes it less likely that the party you're addressing will get defensive when you present your perspective.

2. **State Your Perspective with Clarity and Respect**
   Approach: "I've felt some of the suggestions I've put forward haven't been given much consideration. I believe they could bring value to our project. Can we take a few minutes to discuss them?"
   Why This Works: Using "I" statements focuses on your feelings, rather than placing blame, and creates an opportunity for open dialogue by inviting discussion.

3. **Find Common Ground and Shared Goals**
   Approach: "I know we all want this project to be as successful as possible. My suggestions are based on my research

and experience in this domain, and I think they align with our shared goal of maximizing efficiency."

Why This Works: By highlighting shared goals, you're reminding John and the team of your common purpose. Doing so can encourage them to be more receptive to your ideas. After all, it shows that you're working with the project's best interests at heart.

4. **Collaboratively Propose Solutions**

   Approach: "Perhaps we could allocate some time during our next meeting to brainstorm around these suggestions? I'd also love to hear any feedback or potential improvements. Together, we can refine them to better fit our project's needs."

   Why This Works: Instead of insisting on implementing your ideas as they are, you're inviting collaboration which promotes teamwork. This often leads to more holistic solutions that take into account various perspectives.

By following the Graciously Assertive Communication Model, not only are you advocating for yourself but you're also building stronger team relationships and fostering a collaborative environment. Even when conflicts arise, you can stay focused and not get derailed.

Self-advocacy allows women leaders to build crucial personal relationships with stakeholders, whether the latter are direct reports, peers, or bosses. Personal relationships are crucial because it allows us to build trust. If stakeholders trust you, they will listen to you and become your allies. Allies are important—just as we saw in the courtroom with Juror #1. As we learned from that situation, we all need someone on our side, especially in the corporate world, who has presence and power and can help us gain ground in accomplishing our goals. It is always imperative to observe who in the room has the most power and determine how you can leverage that power to meet your goals.

Scenarios show up every day in business, conference rooms, boardrooms, offices, and teams, and it is up to us as women leaders to identify what needs to be done, persuade, buy, influence, and negotiate to change people's minds. You have to empathize and listen, so that the other party will, in turn, listen to you. This is key, and it should come as no surprise. Empathy is, after all, the Golden Rule, which tells us to do unto others as you would like them to do unto you.

You have to empathize and listen, so that the other party will, in turn, listen to you. This is key, and it should come as no surprise. Empathy is, after all, the Golden Rule, which tells us to do unto others as you would like them to do unto you.

I know that the Graciously Assertive Communication Model works because of personal experience but even more because I've seen it work for thousands of women for many, many years.

Included among those thousands is one of my students, Catalina. She was a senior manager at Mattel, overseeing a team of six direct reports. One of her direct reports, Tonisha, had complained to Catalina during their one-on-one meeting, saying she felt her ideas were consistently overlooked during team meetings. Tonisha also asserted she was not the only person on the team who felt their ideas were regularly overlooked; however, no one was willing to come forward.

After addressing the issue with Tonisha one-on-one, Catalina wanted to determine if any other team members were also feeling their ideas were being overlooked. Addressing the topic right away, she called a team meeting with her six direct reports. She used the Graciously Assertive Communication

Method (GACM) to ensure she created a space for her entire team to have the conversation and to intentionally include everyone in the problem-solving phase.

Once the team had assembled, Catalina took the following steps:

1. **Acknowledge and Empathize**
   Her Approach: Catalina addressed her team honestly. She said, "I've noticed that during our last few meetings, there's been a lot of enthusiasm around certain ideas. I really appreciate the energy everyone's bringing to the table."
   Why It Worked: By acknowledging the group's enthusiasm, Catalina showed she recognized and valued everyone's input.

2. **State Your Perspective with Clarity and Respect**
   Her Approach: Catalina continued, "I feel that some of you may be feeling the suggestions you've put forward haven't been given much consideration. Please know that it was never my intention to make anyone feel this way, and I apologize if what I said or did gave that impression. I would like to have an open discussion about this, so I can learn as well as ensure I don't make anyone else ever feel this way again. I want to be a better leader for all of you. Does anyone want to share?"
   Why It Worked: The use of "I" statements focused on Catalina's feelings rather than making excuses. It also created an opportunity for open dialogue by inviting discussion.

Tonisha spoke up first, sharing with the team that she was reluctant to speak to Catalina about her ideas being overlooked. She then explained how she was pleasantly surprised at how supportive Catalina had been and how quick she was to address the issue. After Tonisha spoke, Catalina went from team member to team member, asking each the same question: "Will you contribute to my growth by sharing with me if I have ever made you feel your ideas were being overlooked?" Catalina's quick action established psychological safety; she was intentionally inclusive of every team member, and this allowed her to build and strengthen trust among her team members.

3. **Find Common Ground and Shared Goals**
   Her Approach: Next, Catalina told her team, "Thank you for your honesty and your contribution to strengthening the trust in our team. I know we all want our team to be as successful as possible. I am committed to ensuring all your ideas are heard. Each of you is an expert in your domain, and I am confident your ideas will continue to align with our shared goal of maximizing efficiency."
   Why It Worked: By highlighting their shared goals, Catalina reminded the team of the common purpose—success for all.

4. **Collaboratively Propose Solutions**
   Her Approach: Finally, Catalina offered a healthy encouragement: "Let's allocate some time during our next meeting to brainstorm how we could ensure everyone's ideas get heard. Together, I am confident we can find solutions to meet our collective goal."
   Why It Worked: Instead of Catalina coming up with a solution on her own, she invited collaboration from her team, promoting teamwork. This would ultimately lead to more holistic solutions that take into account a variety of unique perspectives.

The GACM starts with a fundamental basis: the inherent goodness of humanity. This basis requires us to treat others the way we'd like to be treated. It demands that we become better people. If everyone did this, imagine what a wonderful world we would create.

The GACM starts with a fundamental basis: the inherent goodness of humanity. This basis requires us to treat others the way we'd like to be treated.

The entire Graciously Assertive Communication Model begins with acknowledging and empathizing, and it often requires a pause to hold space, listen, and understand. True empathy is required when we want others to return the same courtesy. Therefore, our communication must always be authentic and honest. When it's not, things will only backfire. You have to surrender your ego, desire to be right, and belief that you know best because there is always more to learn, always something others can teach us. Graciously Assertive communication, at its heart, guides everyone to approach any situation, any conversation, any confrontation, any negotiation, any conflict, any person, any human with understanding and empathy.

It is important for us to move away from responding with our ego and stay in heart in order to keep communication channels open, listen empathetically, and manage our emotions in the process. We may not agree with everything that's on the table or with everything being presented, but we can't allow our emotions to take over. We have to understand, and we have to respect how others feel and what they believe. If we don't listen or try to understand or show we care, we can never influence them or change their minds.

Empathy, after all, is at the heart of influence. When people feel you care about them, they will listen to you and, more importantly, they will trust you.

Empathy, after all, is at the heart of influence. When people feel you care about them, they will listen to you and, more importantly, they will trust you.

Applying the Graciously Assertive Communication Model

1. Acknowledge and Empathize

Here's a list of 25 responses you can use to show understanding, validation, and compassion toward others:

1. I can see how that situation would be challenging.
2. I understand why you might be feeling this way.
3. I appreciate your sharing your thoughts with me.
4. It sounds like you're going through a tough time.
5. Your feelings matter, and I'm here to listen.
6. I'm sorry you're dealing with this right now.
7. I appreciate your honesty in sharing your feelings with me.
8. It's okay to have these feelings.
9. I'm here to support you.
10. I can imagine this situation is really hard for you.
11. You're not alone in feeling this way.
12. I'm here for you, no matter what.
13. I'm grateful you're comfortable talking to me about this.
14. I'm glad you're sharing this with me so we can work through it together.
15. I'm sorry you're having to go through this.
16. I can feel the depth of your emotions, and I'm here to listen and offer support.
17. Your feelings matter, and I'll try to help you navigate them.
18. I can't fully understand, but I want to support you.
19. I'm here to stand by you and help you.
20. You're strong to open up about how you're feeling.
21. I'm here to support you—whatever you're facing.
22. I'm sorry you're feeling this way, but I'm glad you reached out.
23. You're not alone. I'm here to listen.
24. Thank you for trusting me with your feelings.
25. It's okay to feel overwhelmed; I'm here to help you.

Remember: empathy involves truly understanding and connecting with the other person's emotions. It cannot be faked. These phrases can help to get you started, but you need to strive to develop your relationships.

2. State Your Perspective with Clarity and Respect

Here are 25 different ways to graciously state your perspective with clarity and respect, using "I" statements:

1. I want to share my thoughts on this matter in a positive manner.
2. From my standpoint, I see things as . . .
3. I believe it's important to express my viewpoint.
4. I want to offer my perspective with respect.
5. From my perspective, I believe . . .
6. I've given this some thought, and I think . . .
7. I believe my perspective can be constructive.
8. It's my understanding that . . .
9. I'd like to contribute my viewpoint and get your feedback.
10. I feel it's important to communicate my perspective.
11. From my perspective, I believe . . .
12. I think I can add valuable insight.
13. I'd like to express my thoughts.
14. I like to share my thoughts and help us find common ground.
15. I believe it's worth mentioning my perspective.
16. From my interpretation, it seems that . . .
17. I've considered this carefully, and I think . . .
18. I want to communicate my perspective.
19. I believe it's important to share my thoughts in collaboration with you.
20. From my angle, I believe . . .
21. From my interpretation, it appears that . . .

22. I've reflected on this, and I think . . .
23. From my understanding, I think . . .
24. I'd like to offer my perspective in a considerate way.
25. From my experience, I've given this some thought, and I believe . . .

Remember using "I" statements and maintaining a respectful tone are key to effectively communicating your perspective in a gracious and assertive manner.

3. Find Common Ground and Emphasize Shared Goals

Here are 25 different ways a Graciously Assertive Communicator can find common ground and emphasize shared goals while maintaining rapport:

1. Let's focus on our common interests and work from there.
2. I think we can agree on the importance of . . .
3. It's clear we share a common objective in . . .
4. Our mutual goal is to . . .
5. I believe we're both committed to achieving . . .
6. We both have a stake in . . .
7. We can both rally around the idea of . . .
8. It's evident we're aligned in our goal to . . .
9. We're on the same page when it comes to . . .
10. I'm confident we both see the value in . . .
11. We're in sync regarding . . .
12. Our collective aim is to . . .
13. It's apparent our interests converge when it comes to . . .
14. We're united in our pursuit of . . .
15. We're both invested in the success of . . .
16. Our shared aspiration is to . . .
17. I believe we're both striving for . . .
18. We're aligned in wanting to achieve . . .

19. We're working toward the common goal of . . .
20. I think we both recognize the significance of . . .
21. We're both on board with the idea of . . .
22. Our shared mission is to . . .
23. I'm convinced we're both committed to . . .
24. We both agree that . . .
25. We're both striving for the outcome of . . .

Using phrases like these, a Graciously Assertive Communicator can effectively find common ground and emphasize shared goals during conversations, fostering understanding and collaboration.

4. Collaboratively Propose Solutions While Considering All Parties' Concerns

Here are 25 different ways a Graciously Assertive Communicator can collaboratively propose solutions while considering both parties' concerns, aligning with shared goals, and inviting input and ideas:

1. Let's brainstorm some solutions.
2. I'd love to hear your thoughts on potential ways forward.
3. How about we work on finding a solution that meets both our needs?
4. I'm open to exploring options and addressing our concerns.
5. Let's pool our ideas and come up with a solution that works for everyone.
6. I'm interested in hearing your suggestions for resolving this.
7. Can we collaborate on finding a solution that aligns with our shared goals?
8. How can we create an equitable solution?
9. Let's find a win-win solution.
10. I'm eager to work together on a solution with you.

11. Can we brainstorm solutions?
12. Let's find an idea that can bridge the gap between our viewpoints.
13. Let's find a solution that respects our common goal.
14. How can we ensure our solution addresses your needs?
15. I value your input in creating a solution.
16. I'd like to propose a collaborative solution.
17. How about we craft a solution?
18. Let's explore solutions that meet our collective goal.
19. Let's collaborate on a solid solution.
20. Can we work together to find a solution?
21. Let's put our heads together and find a solution that works for both of us.
22. What if we find a solution that meets our common goals?
23. I value your perspective; let's find a solution.
24. What if we devise a solution that incorporates your ideas into the mix?
25. I'm eager to find a solution with you.

Using these phrases, a Graciously Assertive Communicator can effectively propose collaborative solutions that foster a sense of partnership and inclusiveness.

CHAPTER FIVE

THE GRACIOUSLY ASSERTIVE TRANSFORMATION

Everyone has a unique story, filled with moments of joy and sorrow, happiness and melancholy, challenges and triumphs. All can be incredible learning experiences. Some share their stories, others guard them in their hearts and mind, but at the end of the day, every story molds us into the people we are today. The courageous women who come to seek help in my program often find inspiration in other women's stories. As they hear their peers share about their life, they are able to see that they are not alone in their experiences. They are not the only ones whose stories include traumatic origins and pain.

Come along with me as I describe how trauma inhibits women from blossoming as leaders, why it is crucial for them to pinpoint the pain of their past, and how they can overcome it through resilience and community. Their stories testify to their power, resilience in the face of hardship, and inner strength. Join us in this safe space as I share their stories. Be inspired and filled with hope as you discover how the Graciously Assertive Leadership method changed their lives forever. But, before we do this, let's do a quick dive into trauma. I am confident that it may help you recognize your own—and overcome it.

From Trauma to Transformation

Past trauma and lack of emotional healing often impede us from becoming better people. As the saying goes, "Hurt people, hurt people." The Graciously Assertive Lifestyle seeks to resolve past hurts, so women can heal and become better humans and better leaders.

If you are a human being, you have trauma. You may not be aware of your trauma, but trust me, it's there. Leaders have a moral responsibility to become aware of their trauma and self-regulate their behavior. After all, past trauma impacts our ability to communicate effectively and our ability to move forward. To be successful, efficient, and good leaders, we need to understand the ways trauma affects us. Doing so will allow us to heal and not inflict similar trauma on those around us.

Most often, trauma makes it difficult for us to trust others. We simply don't feel safe around people. When we haven't worked through our trauma, we tend to always be "on the defensive" and guarded in our efforts to communicate. In a similar way, our past trauma causes us to "shrink back" from topics, people, and places that trigger our traumatic memories. We steer away from triggering topics or avoid them altogether, but this further hinders our communication efforts.

Trauma leads to challenges in our self-regulation goals, often resulting in outbursts of emotion, emotional shutdowns, or the inability to express emotions appropriately or channel anger properly. Trauma also has negative effects on memory and concentration. Communication is often interrupted by flashbacks or intrusive thoughts of the traumatic event, making focus in any situation a challenge.

Unresolved trauma makes it difficult to open up to others, thus causing a "wall" and a feeling of detachment from family, friends, and even coworkers. Our ability to empathize is then challenged, directly affecting our communication. Trauma also causes dissociation which makes it difficult to remain mindful and present during communication, lowering not only our self-awareness but also our social awareness.

Unresolved trauma makes it difficult to open up to others, thus causing a "wall" and a feeling of detachment from family, friends, and even coworkers. Our ability to empathize is then challenged, directly affecting our communication.

We need to address and work through our trauma, not only to move forward but to also ensure we don't inflict our trauma on others. We can mend what is broken within and rise from the effects of our trauma. The process begins with forgiveness, the key to healing. Most would agree that forgiveness is one of those "easier said than done" circumstances, but while not easy or immediate, we can set our intention to forgive the individual(s) who harmed us. This will help us work toward forgiving—not for them but for ourselves.

While revisiting and working through our trauma, we must remember the goal is healing. We must turn our focus away from hurt, anger, and hatred and toward restoring our mental and emotional health. We may find the answers in counseling, in community, in spiritual practice, or within ourselves—but we have to work toward healing.

Many women who have attended our leadership courses have found healing from their trauma in our supportive and loving community of female leaders. After all, role models play a huge part in our ability to heal and learn to positively respond to life's challenges. Often, people who were meant to be our role models in our early life are the cause of our trauma. So, in order to heal, we must seek alternative role models to guide us forward. From our specially selected alternative role models, we can learn positive behaviors that empower us in our relationships and communication.

Healing trauma requires us to also focus on our reactions (self-regulation and self-love). In doing so, we can improve ourselves and the effect we have on those around us (social awareness). We need to identify our triggers so we can analyze them and then take the next step toward healing. In re-evaluating our feelings and emotions, we can learn to self-regulate and more effectively communicate without inflicting our trauma onto others. We can heal and move forward, taking control of our lives, overcoming our limiting beliefs, and choosing to live differently in how we see and treat ourselves and how we see and treat others. In working through our trauma, we can arrive at the place of self-compassion and zero judgment of others, thus restoring our ability to effectively communicate and build positive, nontoxic relationships.

Dr. Sophia

Sophia, at the age of six, immigrated to the United States from Ecuador with her mother and brothers to reunite with her father, who was already in the States. Her mother treated her harshly in Ecuador, often punishing her by dragging her to the shower and holding her under the stream of water. Her screams and gasps for breath could be heard throughout the neighborhood, and the practice continued after their arrival to the United States. Unsurprisingly, she developed a fear of water and OCD (obsessive-compulsive disorder).

When Sophia was nine years old, a family member sexually abused her for more than a year. She kept this painful secret for years, too ashamed and scared to share it with others. Traumatized, Sophia withdrew into a state of loneliness and isolation. However, in high school, she met a boy and believed she had fallen in love. In her senior year, she dropped out to be with the boy. Soon, however, Sophia discovered the relationship was nothing more than an abusive replay of her childhood trauma. After a year, she broke up with him, and two months later, she discovered she was pregnant. She ended up raising her child as a single mother.

By the time Sophia had become established in her career, she found she was frustrated with both her work and her personal life. She was in a male-dominated environment where she struggled to demonstrate her true value. She was quiet and maintained a back-of-the-room attitude, waiting for people to come to her, which of course seldom happened. Even though she had earned a master's degree in leadership management, she still didn't truly understand what real leadership meant.

When Sophia heard about our women's leadership program, she knew she had to learn more, so she applied. Within the safe environment my program offered, she realized that her past traumatic experiences had negatively impacted her life, preventing her from advocating for herself. Once she became aware of and acknowledged the root cause of her problems, she began to make progress. She understood that even though past events had molded her perspective, they did not and could not define her as a person or a leader. The program also revealed to her that her past experiences were not her fault. This was a huge revelation for her.

Sophia first learned how to treat herself with love—i.e., self-compassion—and then moved on to practicing gracious behavior with others. It wasn't easy, but with effort, she began leading both herself and those around her from a place of empathy and grace. It was a major mindset shift from feeling like she was a victim with flawed values. Now, when managers lashed out and demeaned her worth, she refused to take it as a personal attack. Instead, she began to set strong personal boundaries and held her head high and continued forward with greater determination to be the best person and leader possible.

Today, Sophia is a courageous risk-taker and intrepid explorer, a totally different—and better—human being. She has learned to live and not simply exist, and she shares her positive, confident attitude and energy with everyone with whom she comes into contact.

Most of the leaders we interviewed were shaped by severe trials in their lives, which we call crucibles, an essential element in the process of becoming a leader. Psychologist Abraham Maslow found that tragedy and trauma were the most important human learning experiences leading to self-actualization. Crucibles enable people to learn life is uncertain, and they have limited control. This new reality empowers individuals to challenge old assumptions and understand they must demonstrate personal agency to deal with their world.

Crucibles enable people to learn life is uncertain, and they have limited control. This new reality empowers individuals to challenge old assumptions and understand they must demonstrate personal agency to deal with their world.

Crucibles often launch leaders into despair, crisis, and doubt. In the midst of a crucible, pain and suffering may overwhelm leaders. With sufficient resilience, leaders emerge from despair and become open to introspection that can catalyze major breakthroughs in their development.

In Her Own Words

When I went through Dr. Davidds' leadership program, I was an individual contributor, not formally a "leader" by the corporate definition. I didn't have direct reports. However, as I took a deep dive into the coursework, participated in the in-person monthly meetings on campus, and absorbed all the written literature, I uncovered I was indeed a leader. Dr. Davidds chose the book and field guide *Finding Your True North* by former Medtronic CEO Bill George as a foundational book in her leadership program curriculum. This was intensely thought-provoking and asked questions of me that I had never encountered in other leadership programs.

My journey began with exploring, acknowledging, and embracing my crucible(s). I had NO idea what a crucible was nor was I able to grasp the earth-shattering impact it had on my life. A crucible moment is a turning point, a profound personal experience that impacts the trajectory of your life. Once acknowledged, it becomes a catalyst for introspection, leading to a deeper understanding of your strengths, weaknesses, values, and purpose.

The process of discovering my crucibles was an inward soul journey that cannot be defined as mere revelations or epiphanies, but more of a spiritual awakening of sorts.

Speaking my crucible into the universe and sharing it with other women in my cohort was a significant and pivotal transformational moment in my journey. The sacred safe space that Dr. Davidds has created in the program helped detoxify my soul of everything that had shaped and molded my life's decisions.

There were many pivotal moments in the program. One that stands out was exploring and uncovering my moral compass (the values which steer my life). Were there any? After another deep journey inward, I understood the correlation between my crucibles and my moral compass and that my values were a direct result of my crucibles. It was a beautifully enlightening moment when I discovered and embraced my values of compassion, empathy, grace, and building community born from trauma.

Uncovering and applying my values to my life and letting go and surrendering my crucibles have been liberating. Most importantly, I uncovered I *was* a leader who inspires, motivates, and empowers with the capacity, ability, and passion to transform individuals and organizations.

Though my transformation process began when I went through this soul-healing program, it hasn't stopped there. My metamorphosis continues, and it is cyclical in nature.

I've occasionally experienced former toxic behavioral and belief patterns rearing their ugly heads. However, the liberating gift of my journey is that I now have heightened awareness. I embody a deep understanding and function at a higher level of consciousness about these patterns and limiting beliefs. I understand that they were caused by traumas deeply entrenched in my soul, dominating every decision I made.

From this journey, I have received the beautiful gift of peace. I have peace and joy that my crucibles no longer define me, and therefore they can no longer limit me. I have emerged into a mindset and space of deep gratitude for all my life experiences, regardless of the pain. Connecting the dots between my heart and mind have liberated me from a space of resentment, anger, and pain.

I'll conclude by saying that since graduating from the program, I have been presented with and accepted unlimited growth opportunities. I have graduated with a doctoral degree from my dream school, USC. I have authored a book and have spoken at several national conferences. And this year, I embarked on a journey and am beginning to thrive in a consulting space where I never could have imagined being prior to the program. I am facilitating organizational culture change and focus groups nationally and internationally, both in English and in Spanish, my native language. I'm living a life filled with authenticity, empathy, grace, and compassion. I'm in a synchronous "flow." This transformative inward journey where I now operate from my values of compassion, empathy, grace, and building community has made me a better human being, thus a better leader.

Mia

Mia's mother and father were forced to marry in Guatemala when her mother became pregnant. They separated when she was two years old, and Mia and her younger brother were raised by their mother. When she was five years old, Mia's mother immigrated to the United States, leaving her and her younger brother in the care of their grandmother. It was during this time that Mia was sexually abused by a family member. Years later, when the memory of the abuse returned to haunt her, she feared her mother wouldn't believe her, so she kept it to herself.

When she was eight, Mia and her brother immigrated to the United States to reunite with their mother. Being an undocumented immigrant was traumatizing because it brought shame and complexity into her life, and Mia promised herself to work as hard as she could to make a better life for herself and her family.

She spent her childhood studying, instead of playing with friends or toys, and doing chores, enduring harsh treatment through it all. Her hard work nearly paid off when she was accepted into USC. Sadly, she had to decline admission and a scholarship because she was undocumented. And so, at age 17, she got a job as a bank teller.

The next several years were spent trying to grow her career. Although Mia achieved the position of branch manager when she was 21, she constantly encountered barriers, causing her to make lateral moves instead of progressive ones. She became increasingly frustrated and unhappy. To make matters more difficult, most of her colleagues were older than her and were senior employees, so they didn't take her seriously.

Mia's persistence paid off, however, and she moved up to become regional manager in charge of fifteen branch banks within seven short years. It was at this stage of her career that she came to know another successful woman who held the position she had been pursuing. At first, she idolized her, but soon found their personalities were at odds. This colleague expected Mia to lead according to a leadership model with which she was uncomfortable and even went so far as to tell her she should look for another job.

Frustrated, conflicted, and disappointed, Mia took a demotion back to branch manager. She found another position as a mortgage tech at another bank, where she worked until she was laid off five years later. She then became a project manager at yet another bank, but she found herself playing different roles again just to please those above her. Sadly, she lacked any freedom to lead in the way her heart was telling her was right. She ultimately became more guarded with each passing obstacle until she lost sight of her true self. Although Mia was confident in her abilities, she increasingly felt demoralized and lacked the assertiveness to confront authority.

Finally, Mia applied to my leadership program, hoping she could find some sort of assistance to crawl out of the quagmire in which she felt stuck. At first she was hesitant to open up, but after hearing others share their stories, a sense of relief washed over her, and the panic attacks she had been experiencing on and off for over 20 years dissipated. She could finally breathe. However, this self-reflection took her back to the time when the manager she had idolized had tried forcing her into a mold. This recollection made Mia extremely emotional, and she cried, though not so much for herself as it was for the other woman.

It was in that moment Mia began to think about what she could have done differently in the situation. She realized both she and her previous manager had sensed the same barrier, which prevented them from sharing their true feelings and getting along. As Mia worked to become a Graciously Assertive Leader, she learned to open herself up and encourage others to do the same. This allowed her to build trusting relationships and connect with other people, including her husband whom she realized she had never really gotten to truly know.

Today, Mia feels free, happy, and proud because she has released the emotional chains that held her in bondage. She is more approachable and more confident in her relationships. She has even learned to see those in authority who are not easily approachable as human beings who have their own stories, and she engages in conversation with them instead of throwing up guards. Her personal relationships, especially with her husband and children, have blossomed as she has embraced the Graciously Assertive Lifestyle.

In Her Own Words

My transformation began when I allowed myself to share my story and accept myself for who I am. I started to allow myself to exist in ways that I had never before. I accepted myself for my strength and for my areas of opportunities. I was so much less critical of myself because I had found a gift in my own story.

My transformation began when I allowed myself to share my story and accept myself for who I am.

When I started to allow myself to accept myself for who I am, I was able to do the same for others and embrace their stories. This allowed me to relinquish limiting beliefs—including doubt in myself and my need to please others—and become fully me.

Finally, I was able to tear down the walls I had erected around me to protect myself and show people who I really was. I was now able to connect with myself and connect with others on a whole other level.

Before my transformation, I had very high expectations of myself and was judging myself in every area of my life. In turn, I was judging others and holding them to unreasonable standards. I would become frustrated, and this frustration would become visible in my social and professional interactions. But now, I was different.

New doors started to open up for me.

So, stopping myself from judging others and being controlling really helped me settle into a happier, more positive state. This helped others feel like they could approach me and connect with me. There have been instances where I thought I needed to hold on to certain people in my life, and that was also affecting my experiences. In keeping and staying true to my own values, I realized relationships often don't necessarily need to be long-term. Sometimes, they exist to teach a lesson and to help you on a certain moment in your journey. Once I realized this, I was able to let go and not hold on to things which no longer served me. My energy changed. I began to feel so much more energetic. I began to behave and feel like a real leader who had love and compassion for others. I also began to look for areas in which I could add so much more value.

Knowing I did not have to perform at a certain standard or be someone I wasn't, I was able to improve my personal and professional relationships, including my relationship with my husband and children. In conclusion, I would say the day I decided to no longer control situations or expect anything, I realized my life would be so much easier. Relationships would improve. Opportunities would show up for me because I was no longer trying to do things I thought I needed to do to get to my goal. Instead, I was focusing more on enjoying my experience, my relationships, and the things I did. The feedback I received from my peers was that I had become more loving and accepting of others and less controlling of their actions.

Today, Mia is an exceptional example of the transformation experienced in our leadership program. She now embodies these pillars and is emerging as an inspiring leader in her own right.

The stories of these courageous women reveal the transformative power of self-leadership inherent in resilience, empathy, and self-awareness. They serve as testaments to the potential for profound personal and leadership growth which can emerge from overcoming adversity and embracing Gracious Assertiveness. The principles highlighted in their journeys are central in developing leaders who are not only effective but also compassionate, inclusive, and transformational in their approach. Because they are so powerful, I'd like to share a few more testaments to the Graciously Assertive Transformation, Leadership, and Lifestyle.

In Their Own Words

Rosemary

When I first joined the program, I was not seen as a leader at my job but rather as an employee without a voice. It was incredibly frustrating to be overlooked when it came to leading teams and taking on important projects. That's when a male ally told me about the Dr. Davidds Leadership Program and urged me to sign up. At the time, I was desperate for any guidance that would help me get out of a cubicle and into a leadership position. Little did I know that this program would completely change my perspective about roadblocks and transform my life forever.

Little did I know that this program would completely change my perspective about roadblocks and transform my life forever.

Through the program, I absorbed invaluable strategies for communicating, such as self-awareness, empathy, and negotiating with grace, especially in a male-dominated field. However, what truly struck me was the realization that I lacked critical leadership skills such as self-confidence and was suffering from imposter syndrome. How could anyone believe in me as a leader if I didn't believe in myself? I mustered the courage to approach my director with everything I had learned from the program and was determined to make a change. Thirty minutes later, I walked out of that meeting with a high-profile, multimillion-dollar project. The program had not only equipped me with the skills I needed but had also ignited a fire within me. I was finally ready to step into my role as a leader, and this project was the perfect opportunity to prove myself.

As I dove headfirst into the project, I applied teachings from Dr. Davidds' lectures. My transformation had taken control as I approached every intersection with confidence and grace, knowing I had the ability to successfully carry out this difficult project. Slowly but surely, I began to see the impact of my leadership and felt like a butterfly slowly shedding her cocoon. The team rallied behind me, and together, we achieved remarkable results.

Since completing the Leadership Program in 2018, my journey of self-discovery as a woman and a leader has only deepened. It has become the compass that guides my decisions, fuels my confidence, and ignites my passion for both science and helping others find their passion in science, technology, engineering, and mathematics (STEM). Today, I proudly lead our company's innovation and technical solutions organization. I am the Founder and President of a nonprofit organization dedicated to empowering young girls in underserved communities to find their passion in STEM.

As I reflect on my transformation and the accomplishments that came with the change, I am filled with excitement and anticipation for the upcoming summer when I will graduate with a doctoral degree from a renowned university. Dr. Davidds' program ultimately provided me with the invaluable gift of understanding my life's purpose and inspiring me to take action every day. I know my journey and transformations are far from over. There are still countless opportunities to achieve, develop, and refine. However, with the knowledge and confidence I gained from the program, I am ready to embrace the next chapter of my journey and continue living a purpose-driven life.

Dr. Veronica

In 2019, I attended Dr. Davidds' leadership program's graduation gala and was awestruck by the smiles I saw on each and every graduate and alumnus who took the stage.

As a recipient of the Dr. Yasmin Davidds' Courage in Leadership Award, I am an ambassador and academic advisor for this program. As a person, I am the daughter of immigrants, a single mother, and a college professor of educational leadership and psychology. I am grateful for the many gifts and leadership opportunities this program has given me on my journey of transformation. This program taught me that becoming a better human and better leader starts with an honest assessment of self and purpose. This program paved a way for me to understand leadership differently by finding my leadership purpose among a community of talented female leaders. Learning among like-minded women was a powerful experience that ignited my courage to connect and lead with my authentic self to live a life of service.

As women, we are discouraged from promoting ourselves because our truth is too powerful for others to understand. However, this program gave me a platform to shine in my excellence. My leadership impact has guided me to present statewide, nationally, and globally. I was awarded the 2021 Effective Practitioner Award from the Online Learning Consortium, featured in Telemundo's Mujeres Imparables, and interviewed on several podcasts. I am currently creating the curriculum for the Latinas in Leadership Institute, in collaboration with Latinas in Power and the University of Connecticut.

April

I am a living testament to the power of evolution and personal growth. Just last fall, I found myself in a challenging place, both personally and professionally. At every turn, life was life-ing! I knew I needed "something," and who knew that something would turn out to be Dr. Davidds' Leadership Program.

This has been a transformative journey that's provided me with the support and a safe space I needed to be vulnerable, to undergo my own healing process, and to grow as a leader in every aspect of my life.

I must admit that I was terrified to share a 20-year-old trauma that still held sway over my life. This program, and my incredible sisters, helped me to let go of the shame, embrace the lessons learned, and step into a newfound self-acceptance. Through this program, I've come to understand my experiences don't define me; rather, I can uncover the gifts within those experiences and choose to navigate life with a perspective focused on discovering those gifts.

Whenever I've been asked about my leadership style, I've always identified as a servant leader, someone dedicated to the growth, well-being, and empowerment of others. This program has reaffirmed my commitment to my legacy and mission, particularly in the realm of well-being.

Dr. Carolina

It was in September of 2022 that I had a Zoom interview for Dr. Davidds' Leadership Program. Almost immediately, I felt a strong sense of connection, openness, and belonging, followed by admiration, pride, empathy, and joy. That interview marked the beginning of a life-changing journey; not only was I accepted into the program, but I was awarded a full scholarship. This removed all financial barriers, allowing me to embark in this transformative program.

You see, a couple of years before that interview, I had felt I had "arrived." I had achieved my dreams of education. As a single mom, I was the first in my family to graduate from high school and college. This success led me to pursue my doctoral degree from USC. During that time, I had become a well-established professional, leading USC's corporate social responsibility program for over a decade and serving on the boards of nonprofit organizations.

However, I still felt something was lacking.

As a Latina in a predominantly male corporate culture, I had adopted a persona that obscured my authentic self, and it was hindering me from embracing my power and confidence. While my accomplishments looked impressive on paper, the emotional armor I wore was weighing me down.

Through this program, I began to lead with empathy and compassion in my professional life, fostering unity and trust. My colleagues recognized this shift, nominating me for the USC staff of the month award. In my personal life, embracing my authenticity strengthened my relationships with family, friends, and my partner. The program rekindled my inner light and my legacy, which I use as a mentor, coach, and friend to help others discover their potential. The program became my journey of self-discovery, healing, and embracing my multifaceted identity. It unveiled our collective power as women, forming lifelong bonds and revealing gifts within each of our lived experiences.

Main Takeaways

1. **Overcoming Adversity and Learning from Trauma:** Overcoming adversity, specifically trauma and abuse, is crucial to experiencing spiritual transformation. As the women's unique testimonies demonstrate, trauma can make you stronger.
2. **The Path to Self-Enlightenment and Transformation:** Honestly reflecting on their pasts allows women to recognize their genuine inner strengths. Their transformation is fundamental in their growth as a better human and their development as a better leader.

3. **Cultivation of Emotional Intelligence and Resilience:** As they progressed through each pillar, the women gained a greater understanding of the significance of emotional intelligence and resilience in leadership development. Honing their capabilities in self-regulation, self-compassion, and gratitude allowed them to learn the importance of building genuine relationships and creating positive organizational cultures.

Overcoming adversity, specifically trauma and abuse, is crucial to experiencing spiritual transformation.

4. **Fostering Graciously Assertive Communication:** Their education in the leadership program became a catalyst for these women, which enabled them to enhance their communication skills and develop their leadership style. They learned to establish healthy boundaries and cultivate inclusive, diverse communication and collaboration with their teams. Asserting themselves while also being kind and respectful helped the women find their voices, advocate for themselves, and become leaders in their line of work.
5. **Leadership Impact and Empathetic Influence:** As the testimonies showed, the Graciously Assertive Communication Model allows women to become influential and empathetic leaders. Using their own unique experiences, they learned to positively impact their professional and personal environments and the significance of empathy, compassion, kindness, assertiveness, and accountability.

CHAPTER SIX

MODELING THE GRACIOUSLY ASSERTIVE METHOD

As explained earlier, Graciously Assertive Leadership finds its foundation on 8 Pillars, as well as the organizational guiding principles that work cohesively to create an environment in which leaders and team members can be nurtured and succeed. These guiding principles include emotional safety, radical humility, attention and active listening, acceptance, nonjudgment, compassion, witnessing, and always assuming the best intention.

In this chapter, I would like to introduce two powerhouse women leaders who successfully live the Graciously Assertive Lifestyle. As Graciously Assertive Leaders, they create a safe corporate culture and allow their teams to feel valued, empowered, and inspired, fostering mutual respect and successful collaboration.

Reba Dominski

Reba Dominski is the senior executive vice president and chief social responsibility officer of U.S. Bancorp, and president of the U.S. Bank Foundation. Leading the company's efforts to maximize both social and environmental impacts, she recently led the successful negotiation of the largest community benefits plan in the history of banking—a five-year, $100 billion commitment to increase access to capital in low-to-moderate-income communities, including communities of color.

Before joining U.S. Bancorp in June 2015, she served for 21 years in various leadership capacities at Target Corporation, including sourcing, planning, operations, and merchandising, and later serving on Target's CSR team as senior director of education and community relations, leading Target's $1 billion commitment to education.

Reba currently serves as vice chair on the board of directors for Make-A-Wish America as well as the advisory committee of the Minnesota Business Coalition for Racial Equity. Before beginning her professional career, she earned her BA in English and graduated with honors from the University of Michigan.

In Her Own Words

Yasmin: Tell me your life story and how it has propelled you to become the leader you are today.

Reba: I was born in India and came to the U.S. when I was two years old. I was raised by a single mother in Detroit. My mother hung a poster on the wall of our kitchen, and I read it every day when eating my breakfast. The poster had a quote from Rabindranath Tagore: "I slept and dreamt that life was joy. I awoke and found that life was service. I acted and behold, service was joy."

My mother raised my sister and me with two core values. One was the importance of education—education as a pathway out of poverty, education as a pathway into opportunity. The other was the importance of service. She taught us that no matter what you have, your life should be in service to others. And so, Yasmin, I truly believe this quote and my mother's example are what brought me to the work I do today.

What I have the privilege of doing every day at U.S. Bank is helping more than 70,000 people make decisions that are good for people and good for the planet. I get to help leverage the resources of corporate America—both human resources and financial resources—to help solve some of community's most intractable problems. I believe after over 30 years working in corporate America that we have some of the most valuable resources to help solve problems. So for me, work is a joy. There are tough days and projects, but what always propels me forward is this concept of service as joy.

Yasmin: Why do you think your mother believed one's life should be in service to others?

Reba: My mom was a pediatrician who trained in India and came to the United States to learn Western medicine with the intent of practicing it in rural India. She went back to India, lost my dad, picked up her two daughters, and brought us back to the U.S. to give us a better life. It's the classic immigrant story of parents wanting better for their children. It's interesting, too, that my mom comes from a long line of teachers, doctors, servant leaders. There was a time when my mom had the opportunity to go into private practice in an affluent suburb of Detroit, but she said no, having always wanted to work in the inner city. She ultimately decided to work in a little inner-city clinic, which consisted of some of the most needy patients in the communities she served for more than 50 years.

I believe for most of us, our life story evolves from the way we were brought up. I have a picture of my paternal grandparents by my computer. They started several English-speaking schools in India because they believed in the importance of education in rural communities. Their schools included playgrounds because they knew the importance of play for children; they had libraries because they knew the importance of literacy; and they served free meals for entire families who could not afford to eat. Breakfast, lunch, and dinner were served free at the school, and they also provided adult literacy and education courses at night. Somewhere in my DNA, I believe my mother and her family, and my father and his family, provided me with this intense sense of purpose—an intense focus on living a life bigger than yourself and a life of service. I think I was born with it, and it flourished amid so many amazing role models in my family. I truly believe the most joyous thing you can do in your life is to just live your life in service of others, especially those who need it the most.

Yasmin: What has been the most difficult time or challenge you have faced in your life and what did you learn from this experience? Has this experience made you a better leader and better human being?

Reba: There have been several, and I always try to ask the question, "What did this teach me?" Negotiating U.S. Bank's $100 billion community commitment was a challenging process. At its heart is a commitment to low-to-moderate-income communities and increasing their access to capital. It started with listening to community groups. Senior leaders at U.S. Bank, including our CEO, met with over 200 community leaders listening to what they needed and their experiences in banking. We listened to criticism and feedback, we listened to what they liked and what they didn't. Then we negotiated with these community groups to achieve the commitment goal. It was one of the hardest things I've ever done in my career. It took a long time, lots of back-and-forth, and negotiations for months.

It was all-consuming, and there were so many moments when I didn't know if we were going to get it done, but everything I learned was priceless. The experience reinforced the importance of resilience and getting through the disappointment, working through the challenges, and getting to the next right step. Even if it isn't perfect, even if it isn't the end, just taking that next step forward was key. Our small team worked nonstop just to power through.

In one of our meetings, I paused to tell them about a phrase that kept coming back to me throughout the process: "You always have a knife."

The phrase came from a training class I participated in at Target. The training was about lessons from the military, and a general told a powerful story. There was a young man who parachuted out of an exploding plane, and he landed in the jungle behind enemy lines. He had nothing, so he thought, "I will die. There is no way I will survive this." He thought about his family and his life and began mentally preparing for the end. Then he remembered the small pocketknife he put in his sock every morning. "Aha!" He then used the knife to cut through the cords and foliage and get himself out of the brushes. He used the knife to cut berries off the bushes to sustain himself. He lived. My takeaway is the concept of "I have a knife." I always have something in my tool kit, whether it's another human being, a concept someone mentioned years ago that stayed with me, something I've read in a book, something I've seen on TV, etc. There's always a way to power through. For me, the power of resilience is something I want to share with the world. We are living in such complicated, divisive times and having the resilience to power through is one of the most important things I have ever learned.

The other big lesson I have learned is the importance of listening. I am a very action-oriented woman. I think to be successful in corporate America and many other settings, you must have a strong bent for action. When someone puts a problem in front of me, I immediately go into problem solving. What are we going to do? How are we going to fix it? Whether it's a two-year-old child or an eighty-year-old adult, I want to fix the problem. I want to move to action. The negotiation with community groups that led to our community commitment was an amazing exercise in patience and listening.

The two things that changed profoundly for me as a result of this experience were my commitment to resilience and the importance of listening deeply before taking action.

Yasmin: Do you believe this experience made you a better human being?

Reba: Absolutely. It did. It made me so much more self-aware, aware of my resilience and the need to slow down and listen first.

The other thing that the experience reminded me of is that we can do hard things. When I am scared or struggling or stuck, I sometimes repeat the phrase, "We can do hard things" over and over again. It is a mantra and a reminder.

I had a 29-hour labor with my first child. I think about some of the things we go through, as women, as human beings, and I know we can do hard things. For me, that was another takeaway from all of this, and it did make me a better person. It made me more self-aware of what I do well, of what I need to do better, and it reminded me that I can do hard things. We can all do hard things.

Yasmin: You mentioned the negotiation was at times challenging. How did you manage?

Reba: What I typically did in those moments was step away and, if I could, spent time outside. Whether it was a five-minute break standing and breathing in the sunshine absorbing vitamin D, or taking my dog for a walk for 40 minutes, I stepped away from the challenges and took myself back to nature.

I also know I am my best when I am relational, when I am connected to another human being. Another approach I took to manage was to continue my mentoring sessions even when I felt the need to cancel appointments. When I focused my attention on helping others, it took me out of the anxiety I was feeling. Then I would come back to the challenge with a renewed sense of energy.

Yasmin: Thank you for your honesty and vulnerability because your words are going to help so many women. As women leaders, we all need to understand our peers—women at the highest level—don't have it all figured out but work through it just like everybody else. We all have different tools we use, and it's okay; it's being human.

Reba: It is being human. Two other tips I use: When you're working on something big, break it into smaller pieces so it doesn't feel so overwhelming. When you have a big task, you wake up every day feeling like you have to figure it all out, but working through singular issues will help make it easier. When facing big challenges, breaking it down into small pieces helps tremendously.

The other tip is to ask for help. So often, as women, we feel we have to have all the answers and as we look at successful women around us, we stand in awe because they have it together, they speak eloquently, they know their business, they stand up for themselves, they're courageous. It is hard not to compare yourself and ask, "How does she have this all figured out?" The reality is that I am a mess in a dress most days. If we can help each other out and lift each other up, let's do it. If you need help, raise your hand and ask. I sit at the top leadership table at U.S. Bank, and I still, on occasion, have to say to my boss, "I don't know how to do this. How would you approach this? I need help."

If we can help each other out and lift each other up, let's do it. If you need help, raise your hand and ask.

Yasmin: So many women feel they can't ask for help because they'll be looked at as less capable or competent. Have you ever felt like this?

Reba: Yes, especially earlier in my career. The higher I go in the organization, the more I realize confidence comes from competence. Without asking for help, I would not be competent. I'll give you an example. When I first got to the bank, I was relatively new to banking. I was presenting at a board meeting, planning to discuss some of the work a partner was leading around tax credits. I called him and said, "I am going to ask you what you might think is a basic question, but I need to know because I'm presenting it to the board of directors. If someone asks, I want to make sure I can answer and do justice to the work you and your team lead. What is a tax credit and how does it work?" As he explained it to me, I took copious notes, which I still refer to today since it's not as easy as it sounds. Then he said, "Thank you so much for asking me that." Most human beings want to feel valued, want to coach, want to give. More often than not, the people I ask for help, like my boss, are excited when I ask. They're excited to help you learn, to help you grow.

Yasmin: Do you believe being a better human being makes you a better leader?

Reba: I don't see how to separate the two. How do you separate being human from anything you are? Being a better human being makes you a better parent. Being a better human being makes you a better spouse or partner. Being a better human being makes you a better friend. Being a better human being makes you a better listener. I think leadership and humanity are inseparable and integrally connected. So my answer is yes, being a better human being has unequivocally made me a better leader. I get lessons every single day on how to be a better human being, and I apply those to my leadership every day.

Yasmin: You have been identified as a Graciously Assertive Leader based on the 8 Pillars of Graciously Assertive Leadership I created. Which of the pillars do you identify most with?

Reba: The three I associate with the most are self-awareness, social awareness, and gratitude. I'm a work in progress around self-regulation, self-compassion, zero tolerance for judgment, and Graciously Assertive communication. I need to work on setting healthy boundaries.

Yasmin: I love that you own you have a long way to go. Where do you struggle?

Reba: I struggle in drawing a line between work and home. We live in a 24/7 world where we are always connected, and I'm a very action-oriented person. If I look at my phone and see emails in my Outlook, I am conditioned to open and answer them. It might be in the middle of a conversation with the human I love the most. It might be in the middle of texting a friend who is in dire straits and needs my advice. And most of the time, it is not even an important work email.

I have been consciously working on this since the pandemic, because during that time, work-life balance and boundaries became even harder. You were home, you were working, always working, it seemed. My team and I experimented with this and committed to making one or two changes to help set healthy boundaries. The one that was effective for me was, at the end of the week, shutting down my laptop and closing the lid. It's usually combined with pouring a glass of white wine, which signals for me that the week is over, the work is done, and I now belong to the people I love so much.

My CEO will send me an email, and I think I have to answer right away, but then I ask myself, "Do I really believe the CEO of a Fortune 150 company is sitting there going, 'Boy, if Reba doesn't respond in the next minute, I don't know what I'm going to do'?"

Much of it, for those of us who are driven and motivated, is self-imposed. For me, it is as simple as closing the laptop and turning my phone over. I have turned off notifications on social media because it was a distraction. So, I'm working on healthy boundaries, adding a new technique every few months. Sometimes it succeeds, sometimes it fails, but I am trying. It is a constant battle for me, but I'm getting better.

Yasmin: You are a Graciously Assertive Communicator which means you're able to hold people accountable while simultaneously holding space for them—has this come naturally for you or have you had to cultivate it?

Reba: Caring for others has always come naturally to me, but I also am very driven and drawn to the business. I have had to moderate my behavior to make sure the people I do care about know I care about them, and I'm listening to them. Every week or two, I meet with my direct reports for a one-on-one conversation. I recall a situation where I went right into business, and toward the end of the conversation, I remembered her mother just had surgery last week, and I should ask about it.

To address the opportunity, I made a change that has been very helpful. Now, I start my one-on-one meetings with two questions, the first being, "How are you coming to this conversation?" Sometimes they answer, "I'm ready to go. I'm ready to talk about the business." Sometimes it's, "Boy, I've had a hard week, or I had a rough weekend." It gives me a moment to listen and prioritize their feelings over what needs to get done.

The second question is, "What's top of mind for you today?" While I have things that are top of mind for me, this says to them, "This is your time. I am here to listen to you and to be as helpful as I can be."

The beautiful thing about these two questions is it allows me to quickly move into coaching and feedback. I have an amazing group of leaders who work for me. They don't need much from me, but sometimes they need a little bit of help, a little bit of coaching and guidance. Sometimes I need to remove an obstacle. Most people want feedback, they want to know where they stand. They want to be coached. They want to be guided. To me, coaching, feedback, and guidance are some of the most gracious and kind things you can do for other people.

I've always been a kind person. I'm passionate about kindness, and I feel showing kindness should be valued in corporate America. Kindness gets results. Kindness can deliver tough messages and still leave human beings intact. Kindness is the mother of empathy, and empathy is essential to any honest, productive, open dialogue.

I'm passionate about kindness, and I feel showing kindness should be valued in corporate America. Kindness gets results.

I once had a boss, not at U.S. Bank, who told me in my mid-year review, "People like you too much. Everyone likes you. I want one person here to hate you by the end of the year."

It was one of those crucible moments for me, and I walked away and said, "If I actually have to be hated to be successful at my job, I don't think this is the right place for me."

The same day, I was at one of my daughter's pediatric appointments and I read a quote in *Real Simple* magazine—"You need to be an apple pie, soft on the inside, but with a thicker outer crust." In that moment I realized I had never shown this boss the side of me that did give tough feedback. I'm very direct with people, but I do it in a way that is right for me and doesn't leave the other person feeling like they couldn't be coached and do better.

I started showing him examples by forwarding emails and saying, "Oh, by the way, I want you to see how I handled this situation with a vendor." I did it to show him you can be kind and be very successful in corporate America. I think some of the most successful people in corporate America are some of the kindest. I am on this mission around kindness to ensure kindness is seen as a positive for business leaders.

Yasmin: You have a strong ability to pivot when receiving negative feedback, not allowing the feedback to set you back. What allowed you to pivot, bounce back, and move to action?

Reba: It was not easy and I was confused, but it's resilience that says, "Okay, I got this information. I can't ignore it. I need to do something." Resilience drives me to move forward. I want to get through it, but I want to do it in a way that's right for me.

Always show yourself grace. Start with being kind to yourself. Give yourself time to be hurt. Give yourself time to be angry. Give yourself time to be confused. Give yourself time to grieve. The world is not fair. This is not okay. Someone misunderstood me, someone did me wrong. Take your time, get through it, and then kick yourself in the butt and say, "Okay, now what am I going to do about it?"

That's when resilience pays off, creativity pays off. I didn't have to do it the way he said. I didn't agree to make someone hate me by the end of the year. I never said anything to him. I just started showing him, and by the end of the year, it wasn't an issue.

Yasmin: You have the ability to not stay in mental negative space when receiving disappointing personal feedback. Is there a childhood experience that taught you how to get unstuck quickly?

Reba: There were a lot of challenges and sadness in my childhood. My dad died by suicide when I was two and my sister was five. It was the reason we came to this country. I'm an advocate for mental health and mental health awareness and bringing these issues into the light. I believe the next generation is going to do that in a beautiful way. I think my resilience comes from my ability to work through grief, to work through trauma. It is combined with my sense of ridiculous optimism and positivity. Something in that mix of grief, trauma, and positivity led to the resilience I have, the ability to find a way through it.

Yasmin: In terms of organizational leadership, how do you deal with failure?

Reba: I don't use the word failure typically because the word is heavy and carries a lot of weight. Failure is such a heavy burden to put on someone. To me, it's all about learning. At U.S. Bank, we approach things with agile methodology. You're always getting feedback. You're always thinking about how you can improve. Whether it's a product, a service, or your development, the question is always, "How can I improve myself?" You're never done. You're always trying. It's not about failure; it's about the journey. My favorite quote is from the great Maya Angelou: "Once you know better, then you do better," and that's how I live my life. It's not about failure. It's about knowing better and doing better.

Yasmin: What happens when you have laid out your plans with your team, and for whatever reason they haven't been able to deliver? How do you regroup and re-inspire people to double their efforts and move forward?

Reba: Some of it comes back to setting clear expectations up front. For example, when I first came to U.S. Bank, I was charged with creating a platform for a giving engagement. I was given resources to create a strategic vision for giving and philanthropy in six months. It was a challenge, and as I worked on it, I realized I was working with a group of perfectionists, of which I was one. We came up with a mantra, "Progress, not perfection."

When I think about the people who have given me the best moments of, "Oh, boy, this isn't right. We've got to do something different," it's usually someone who just makes a comment that stays with you. We had a big employee engagement activation planned. It was close to being done, when this young woman on my team said, "I don't think it's going to work." She very clearly told me why. And she was right. I went, "Oh, my gosh, you're right." I think she felt horrible, but I thanked her. "I don't know what we're going to do, but thank you so much for having the courage to say what needed to be said." We rolled up our sleeves and worked all night and got it fixed. I would so much rather address it up front and know about it before it gets rolled out to 70,000 people.

The other thing I try to do is reward those who have the courage to speak up. At U.S. Bank, we also encourage leaders who listen up. I think it is the key is making sure your team feels comfortable saying something's not right and knowing their leader will listen.

Yasmin: Who are the people you most admire when it comes to leadership, and why?

Reba: I have been blessed to work with some amazing leaders. My first director at Target is a dear friend who had incredible creativity and an overarching sense of humor. I took that from her. From the head of sourcing at Target, I took strategy and thoughtfulness. She was the most strategic and thoughtful leader I've ever worked with.

From the head of CSR at Target, I took presence and preparation. I watched how she prepared whenever she spoke, and it was an incredibly valuable lesson. My first boss at U.S. Bank showed me authenticity and courage. She was a change agent and from her I learned to be a change agent in financial services, which is not easy to do. My current boss at U.S. Bank is incredibly calm and balanced and does an outstanding job of listening first. He is always open to having a conversation when I bring him a challenge. I loved this, and I picked it up.

My first CEO at U.S. Bank treated everyone as if they were the only person in the room. Whether he was talking with a teller or an executive, he always gave the person he was addressing his full attention. It is a gift, and something I've tried to observe and absorb from him. My current CEO has taught me the power of clear and concise communication, which is a gift that just continues to give.

I have so many amazing leaders in my life, and it all started with my mother. My mother will always be my hero, my number one leader and example. From her, I learned the world is bigger than myself, and that by focusing on others, you can derive a profoundly meaningful life and a lot of joy.

Yasmin: What are your last thoughts you would like to share with our fabulous readers?

Reba: Be kind, be yourself, and be present.

Keetha Mills

Keetha Mills is President and Chief Executive Officer of the Foundation for California Community Colleges (FoundationCCC). Since 2012, she has led FoundationCCC as a non-profit auxiliary partner to the California Community Colleges, the largest system of higher education in the nation. As a community college alumna, Mills understands the value of a community college experience and the power that education has to change lives. She has guided the organization to achieve steady and sustainable growth in providing more than $165 million in annual resources to students, colleges, and communities.

Mills has nearly 30 years of experience in executive leadership, nonprofit management, finance, accounting, and operations. Before joining the Foundation, she was Chief Operating Officer and Chief Financial Officer for Planned Parenthood of Houston and Southeast Texas, and the Interim CEO of Planned Parenthood of Louisiana and the Mississippi Delta. She managed a $490 million portfolio for Hines Interest Limited Partnership and worked for Arthur Andersen and PricewaterhouseCoopers. Mills also acted in an executive leadership role at Dynegy, an S&P 500 company.

Mills holds an associate of arts degree in business administration from Lee College in Baytown, Texas, and a bachelor of science degree in accounting from the University of Houston. In addition to her role on the Board of Directors of HEAL Trafficking, she also currently serves on the California Lottery Commission, maximizing supplemental funding to the state's public education systems.

In Her Own Words

Dr. Yasmin: Tell me your life story and how has it propelled you to become the leader you are.

Keetha: Growing up, great things and happy moments happen to you, but they are intertwined with equally traumatic moments. As a child, there were many times I felt inadequate or not good enough.

My parents' marriage was not a happy one. I recall there was always fighting and discord. And so, I always made sure that I would always be in a place where I can get out of a difficult situation. My childhood ultimately instilled a fierce independence, tenacity, and grit in me. I remember thinking that I will take care of myself because nobody can take care of me any better than I can.

Another thing I learned from my childhood is the importance of health and its connection to self-care. I never take my health for granted. My parents both had significant health issues. My father was a disabled veteran who took a bullet to his head, lost the use of his left arm, and had paralysis in his left leg. My mom was diagnosed with diabetes as a teenager. She had to get up and give herself a shot every morning and really regulate her diet. As a kid, you don't really realize the impact this has on you. You think it's normal. But as I got older, I realized health is so important.

Another influential moment in my life comes from an interaction I had with my mother when I was nine or ten years old. My mother was a fifth grade schoolteacher in Texas who loved her kids and her job, but she felt she was never paid her worth. She never felt her salary could sustain the lifestyle she wanted for us. She always wanted better for me. I have this vivid memory of being at a party with my mom. Her friend walked up, and started talking to me, saying, "Keetha, what do you want to be when you grow up?"

I looked up, beaming with pride at my mother, and said, "I want to be a teacher."

To my shock, my mother pointed her finger at me and angrily said, "No, you don't."

I will never forget that moment. I cried for an hour, wondering, *Oh my God, what did I do wrong?*

My mother later explained, "I want better for you. I want different from you. You are smarter. You can do so many things. You can be whatever you want. But you don't want to be a teacher. I want you to think bigger than I did. I want you to do more than what I did." Her words had a huge influence on me and helped me in my decision process. I chose to become an accountant because I was good at math. I didn't really know what an accountant was, but I knew it wasn't a teacher. I thought it would make my mom proud, and I looked forward to the prospect of working in a big city in a high-rise. When I recall our conversation today, I realize that it was always my desire to achieve bigger, better, and bolder things and serve more people.

Although I ended up not being a teacher, I had so much admiration for the work my mother did and how she loved her students. Growing up, she'd bring her students home, and we'd all hang out together; they were like part of our family. She was committed to helping her students succeed and that stuck with me as well. I love that I've come full circle back to education. I went through the corporate world, worked in oil and gas, in healthcare, and came full circle back to education. It has allowed me to have a career that I feel really good about and honors my mom. We all, at the end of the day, want to make our mommies proud.

Dr. Yasmin: What has been the most difficult time and greatest challenge you have faced in your life? What did you learn from it, and how has it made you a better human being?

Keetha: My later college and early career years were very challenging, particularly getting out of my own way, getting out of my head, and coming out of my shell. I was an only child, and this has shaped my leadership style. Being an only child was a blessing and a challenge. I learned how to be alone, how to love myself, and how to create on my own. However, it also made me a bit too comfortable with being alone.

I was so driven in college because college was a means to an end. It was how I would achieve my goal of being something other than a teacher, making my mom proud, and being independent. My first two years were spent in a community college, which was an amazing time in my life and cost-effective. However, it was not a traditional college experience. I was working full-time, paying for my tuition and going to school from 6:00 p.m. to 10:00 p.m. The days were full, and I was committed to both working and getting my education. When I transferred to a four-year university, I knew I was getting close. I asked myself, *What do I want to do?* Soon, I began to realize that I needed to come out of my shell and that my good grades weren't enough. I ended up deciding to go into public accounting and work for Arthur Andersen. And so, I forced myself to carve out what little free time I had and put myself out there. I joined clubs, volunteered, and became president of two of the three clubs. It was insane!

I ran myself ragged for years, then I got my dream job at Arthur Andersen. I was on top of the world, but I still faced a lot of self-doubt. *You got your dream job*, I thought. I did all the things, it worked, but now I was back at the bottom, still Keetha, the girl who came from a small town and went to community college. Everyone around you went to great schools. Plagued by feelings of not being good enough, I poured myself into my work and was promoted in a year and a half. It was then I realized I had to slow down, or I would kill myself. I asked myself, *What is it all for if I can't stop and breathe and enjoy these moments of success?*

Unable to appreciate my successes and always chasing the next big thing, I got sick all the time. Realizing I needed to stop and smell the roses was super transformational for me. In my moment of transformational awareness, a lot changed but it didn't happen overnight. I knew I needed to stop, to breathe, to do things differently. I asked myself, *What's the first step? What makes you happy? What do I need to bring into my life to bring more joy, to celebrate?*

I realized my health was a big trigger. Remember, my parents didn't enjoy good health, and this made me feel very strongly about mine. I didn't want to take it for granted, so I started working out and eating better. It brought me joy. I realized I loved the great outdoors, and I also began playing tennis. I wasn't very good but being outside made me happy. I started hiking, I discovered I enjoyed travel. The big change was taking stock of what brought me joy and doing it! I knew no one would fix it for me and that I was the only one who could fix it and make it better. I had to find what made me happy and make time for those things.

Dr. Yasmin: Do you believe that experience has made you a better leader overall?

Keetha: One thousand percent—but it has been an evolution. It didn't make me a better leader right away. Focusing on what made me happy made me a better person. Over time, I made these things habits, realizing what a difference they made. I understood I had done it for myself, and I needed to give other people the grace and permission to do these same things so they could become better themselves and show up at work. This ultimately allowed me to help others up so they too could find joy and happiness in their careers and their lives.

Dr. Yasmin: Do you believe becoming a better human being makes you a better leader?

Keetha: If you're not happy, no one around you is happy. It seeps into everything. It seeps into your mood. It seeps into how you interact with others. It seeps into how you treat people, your communication, your outlook on the world. Having a joyful attitude makes you a better leader because it *shows.* People can feel it, people can hear it, people can see it. Being a better person permeates everything around you.

Having a joyful attitude makes you a better leader because it *shows*. People can feel it, people can hear it, people can see it. Being a better person permeates everything around you.

Dr. Yasmin: You have been identified as a Graciously Assertive Leader based on my 8 Pillars of Graciously Assertive Leadership. Which of the pillars do you identify most with and why?

Keetha: Several of these pillars really resonate with me. Self-awareness is super important to me. I can't have joy in my life every single day without being aware when I'm feeling off. I have to make sure people around me know I'm aware of it, forgive myself, and move on. This also leads into self-compassion, which is a hard muscle to build. I try to give myself the time and grace to make mistakes, as well as do the things I love. It all pays off and makes me a better leader and person.

I also live by gratitude. I'm so grateful for the role I play in supporting higher education, positively impacting millions of students, and being surrounded by my passionate team of professionals. It all fills my heart with gratitude and love and brings me joy. It helps me show up as a better leader. I love my life. I'm fulfilled by every aspect of it. I am full of gratitude.

Dr. Yasmin: Are there pillars that you struggle with or really want to build upon?

Keetha: I struggle with social awareness and self-regulation. I think it comes back to the voice in my head: *I'm just Keetha from a small town who went to community college.* I really try to surround myself with smart people, who know different things than I know. I find I get really frustrated if people who are smarter than me don't understand something. I have to be careful not to judge, thinking, *If I know this, you should know this.* I have to catch myself and ensure that I give others space and time to get there with me.

Dr. Yasmin: A Graciously Assertive Leader is one who is direct and honest, yet kind and empathetic of the feeling and needs of others. Do you feel you have always been a Graciously Assertive Leader?

Keetha: I feel like I have *grown* into a Graciously Assertive Leader. As an only child, it was often all about me. I was my parents' little princess. We didn't have a lot, but I always had everything I needed and wanted. Growing up in that kind of environment can make you very selfish. I didn't have any control over it—I was just a kid being raised by parents who put me on a pedestal—and so I had to unlearn much of what being an only child taught me. I had to start understanding there were other people around me. Slowly, I became more self-aware and started to correct my selfish behaviors. Had I not had those realizations early in life, I would not have become as successful as I am today.

Dr. Yasmin: Has being a Graciously Assertive Leader helped you lead in a better way?

Keetha: Absolutely, the work we do is 1000% mission-driven. People come to work for the foundation because they believe in what we do and are passionate about helping students, showing grace and understanding, and giving support no matter what their lived experience has been so far. They are here because they want to lift up and create better lives for themselves, for their families, and for their communities. We have to provide the support to help them succeed. Just being a good person isn't enough; true leadership is going above

Just being a good person isn't enough; true leadership is going above and beyond and showing up in a way that is gracious, kind, and forgiving.

and beyond and showing up in a way that is gracious, kind, and forgiving. This is the secret sauce for our success.

Dr. Yasmin: As a leader, why is being both gracious and assertive important?

Keetha: Being gracious in the process and assertive in decision-making are important. At the foundation, I am proud of our culture of shared leadership because it empowers leaders at all levels of the organization to really flex their knowledge muscle and their leadership muscle, no matter where they sit in the organization. Shared leadership gives team members the courage to speak up and be assertive. We're hiring really smart people who are experts in their fields and know their programs, services, and area of expertise better than anyone around them.

The culture of shared leadership has strong tenets of collaboration, teamwork, and working together—not just within the team but across teams. Shared leadership requires grace and empathy because it welcomes all the voices to the table. However, as a leader, you also have to be assertive and say, "Okay, we've now talked it out, heard all the differing views, and they have all been good. We've gotten to a better answer, and this is what we're going to do to move forward."

Having grace, empathy, and patience, and valuing the time it takes to bring all the relevant voices, opinions, and directions to the table are crucial. But then being able to be assertive enough to say, "This is the decision we're going with, but we can pivot along the way if needed" is equally important. Assertiveness paired with grace and empathy is key.

Assertiveness paired with grace and empathy is key.

Dr. Yasmin: Do you believe your Graciously Assertive Leadership style has helped you be a more effective communicator?

Keetha: Absolutely. It's also made me be a better listener. I believe listening is a huge part of being a good communicator. If I have to be the one who answers every question or states my opinion first, it changes the whole dynamic of the conversation. A major part of graciousness is taking a pause, breathing, and listening. It's not being the first voice around the table every time but making sure your voice is heard in the right place and at the right time. It's about giving time and space for others to express their views and their opinions.

A major part of graciousness is taking a pause, breathing, and listening. It's not being the first voice around the table every time but making sure your voice is heard in the right place and at the right time.

Dr. Yasmin: In terms of organizational leadership, how do you deal with failure?

Keetha: Failure is hard. None of us wants it, none of us likes it, and it doesn't feel good. However, I believe failure is a gift. It's where you learn the most. When you succeed, you rarely take the time to identify what made you succeed and learn from it. When you fail, you can take the opportunity to ask yourself, *What happened? What do we learn from this? What worked well? What can we do differently*? We need to be able to tease out the good parts and move them forward and identify the bad parts and leave those behind. When I reflect on my time in our organization, I realize that our failures are some of the things I'm most proud of. This is because we were able to work together to figure out what didn't work and come up with a solution to transform our programs into something extraordinary.

For example, our student ambassador program started as a government-funded statewide program that utilized student volunteers. At first, we thought that this was perfect for us. It was new, unlike anything community colleges had done before. But when we drove in, we quickly realized there was way too much red tape. The cost model did not cover for the costs of the program, so we were losing our shorts and failing miserably. We recruited students, and they would leave. It wasn't sustainable. And so, we had to stop and move out of that grant. During our post-mortem, we agreed there were many great things about the program. It engaged students locally, having them work/volunteer and get resources out to their peers. We then realized that if it was funded by philanthropy, all the red tape would be gone.

We started out with 10-15 student ambassadors. We soon hit our milestone of serving 1,000 student ambassadors over the past few years, and it's now this robust program. We're working with 100-plus students a year, and they're working out in their communities. Philanthropy loves it. We're able to attract funding, and it all started from failure—the grant that was not working. We salvaged the good parts and turned it into something that is now thriving and growing. Failure can be a real superpower.

Dr. Yasmin: I want to capture the moment here. You utilized a "failed project," took the good out of it, pivoted, leveraged it, and built upon it to make something great. As the CEO of this foundation, you're known for having transformed and sustainably built it to four times its size in twelve years. How did you do it?

Keetha: When I became CEO, we were worth around $40 million, and today we are celebrating an annual budget of $165 million. It's been a transformational change. I began 15 years ago as the Chief Financial Officer, a position in which I served for three years. When I moved into the CEO role, we were about 10 years old. We had gone from this scrappy, small nonprofit to a conglomerate of 15 to 20 different programs and services. We were a bunch of great, little programs, but they were just stuck together and were not really working together as a team. I wanted to make them a cohesive unit in which every piece was working together.

I came across this article on shared leadership, and it really spoke to me. It was all about collaboration, teamwork, cross-collaboration, as well as the empowerment of leaders, all the incredibly smart, talented people who knew their business like no one else. Shared leadership, I realized, would allow everyone to play off of one another and get even smarter while making the programs stronger and more effective.

It was the era of getting the house in order—identifying all those really smart people and getting them in the right seats. Some needed to elevate, some needed to move on. I didn't need to be surrounded by a bunch of Keethas. I needed to be surrounded by those who knew things I didn't, those who were smarter than me, those who had skills I lacked. We spent the first three to five years of my CEO role really getting the house in order.

Once we got the house in order, we knew it was work in process. We gave ourselves permission to go. We had the right people. We were doing amazing work. But now we needed a big goal. Where were we going? We were at $50 million. We were growing incrementally. We were poised and had momentum, so we set our goal to double our impact to $100 million. It was less about the number and more about the impact. We felt bold and audacious, but we knew we had some small programs that needed to think bigger. We had some big programs that needed to think bigger. Everyone needed to think about how to double our impact and create more outcomes for students. We set a goal to hit double impact by 2028. We hit the goal three years after we set it. We were at $135 million. It was all about opening our minds and giving ourselves the permission and the framework to think about growth, not for growth's sake but for our students, our colleges, our communities. We tripled down on new ideas—climate, AI, all things we should and could be doing that but hadn't thought about—and changed our mindset. This was hugely transformational for us.

Dr. Yasmin: What happens when you have laid out your plan with your team and—for whatever reason—they haven't been able to deliver? How do you regroup and reinspire people to move forward?

Keetha: This is the place where our culture of shared leadership shines because we create high accountability for ourselves, and we expect accountability from each other. When things aren't moving, we all feel it, and we want to figure out what is stuck and how we can free ourselves so we can move forward.

We have weekly executive team meetings where we come together and problem solve. We have quarterly strategy sessions. When things aren't moving, they go on the executive team agenda, and we talk it out as a team, not behind each other's backs. If it's really sticky, we put it on for a quarterly retreat agenda and really dig into it and bring other people who need to be at the table. It's really about creating that environment of trust where we can name what isn't working, spread awareness, and problem solve. There is no blaming and shaming. It is Graciously Assertive problem solving. It has to be done right, in a safe space, so people feel safe to speak up and collaborate. The first step is realizing you have a problem, identifying what exactly that problem is, and then being able to talk about it and solve the problem with the best heads around the table.

Dr. Yasmin: What areas of your leadership style do you wish you could be better at?

Keetha: I struggle with coming out from behind the curtain and being more face-forward. I am working on being comfortable working the rooms and being the CEO, front and center. In some ways, this quirk of mine makes the foundation perfect for me because, as a supporting organization, it's not a place where it is always appropriate for me to be front and center every time. There are times when it is, but the chancellor is the face, and we are there to support and uplift our chancellor, our system office, our colleges, and our students. That balance is really good for me.

Dr. Yasmin: Who are the people you most admire when it comes to leadership, and why do you admire them? What influence have those people had on you?

Keetha: I have deep admiration for one of my partners at PricewaterhouseCoopers, Bill Barley. Public accounting is tough, grueling, and very much an individual sport. You're working in teams, but it's all about you and getting promoted. The hours are insane as you jump from client to client. At one point in my life, I was a staff person and had no office. One day, I was sitting at my little desk working in the pits when Bill Barley comes out of his beautiful corner office, walks right up to me and says, "Keetha, I just wanted to come say thank you. I know you've been working really hard, and I really appreciate all you've done." Everyone was silent. I almost fell out of my chair. I was blown away. It showed me the power of gratitude. I realized I had never heard the words "thank you" in my entire career in public accounting. I'm forever indebted to him for that because it made me realize that I had never heard the words because I had never used the words *myself* with my team. I realized then and there that I had to voice my gratitude for my team members more often.

I also learned a lot from leaders I did not admire. They taught me what not to do. They were influential leaders, but working for them was hard. It was with them that I leaned into my grit and tenacity to power through challenges. I also relied on my analytical brain to identify what was totally wrong and inappropriate and what I promised to never do as a leader. I think those leaders were just as impactful—if not more—as those from whom I learned all the good leadership traits.

Dr. Yasmin: Is there anything else you would like to share with readers?

Keetha: Always be curious because curiosity creates incredible learning experiences. I knew accounting and finance were not my passion, and I was really curious about marketing, communications, and merchandising. People love to talk about what they do, and it was a way for me to get out of my shell and meet people I wouldn't have otherwise met and learned from.

I'd also recommend volunteering. It's a great way to learn and gain exposure to different areas of the business. Curiosity can be a real superpower because it can help you excel and advance but also learn more about where your passion lies and what is most interesting to you. So, flex your curiosity muscle. Don't be afraid to talk to people or to ask them about their work, their role, and themselves. It is a really powerful tool.

Common Threads

In these interviews, we see the many common threads that connect Graciously Assertive Leaders. They all share a unique vision of the world, life, and humanity. They are all self-aware, learn from their experiences, and have come to terms with their trauma. They live from a place of gratitude and have a mindset of growth and positivity. They see Graciously Assertive Living as a superpower. They know how to create safe spaces and have the resilience to bounce back, reframe their situations, learn from their failures, and do better. They demonstrate empathy and the value of kindness, and they see constructive feedback as valuable learning.

CHAPTER SEVEN

WORKPLACE COMMUNICATION AND AVOIDING UNGRACIOUS BEHAVIORS

Let's define ungracious behavior at work and answer this pressing question: "Is there pressure on women to be perfect in business?" A quick internet search of "ungracious behavior at work" turns up "verbal harassment" as a classic example. Interesting, isn't it?

Ungracious behavior is the opposite of what we have been learning; in fact, it is toxic, and it leads to instability in the workplace. A recent study published in MIT Sloan Management Review demonstrates how companies are failing women because women are 41% more likely to experience toxic culture in the workplace.[12] It is not surprising; ungracious behavior breeds an unhealthy culture. It is most often perpetrated by disrespectful leaders who define company culture and thus undermine employees.

The MIT Sloan study identifies elements of toxic culture including but not limited to: gender inequity, sexual bias, racism, lack of inclusivity, lack of respect, favoritism, microaggression, gaslighting, bullying, and other unethical behaviors.[13] The findings in this study align with my own research among the 1,000 participants of the Dr. Yasmin Davidds Leadership Institute.

Our research has shown that corporate culture, compared to academia, nonprofits, and government, is most oppressive to women and is known to cause the most workplace trauma. Why is this the case? Well, academic, nonprofit, and government work is tied to altruism. It involves the betterment of people and causes greater than oneself. This greater purpose allows employees to build resilience, feel safer, and behave with kindness and compassion. The primary focus of corporations, however, is on profit. This makes it difficult for women to feel a sense of purpose or that they are truly contributing to the betterment of society. Our research shows that corporate women struggle with their self-confidence and self-worth more than women in other industries and areas.

Women in the corporate financial sector, even at the highest level, struggle most with imposter syndrome: the belief that they are undeserving of their achievements and the high esteem in which they are held.[14] Many say they rarely spoke of or recongnize this inhibiting phenomenon in themselves until they entered our leadership program.[15]

Women in the corporate financial sector, even at the highest level, struggle most with imposter syndrome: the belief that they are undeserving of their achievements and the high esteem in which they are held.

According to our research, traditional leadership programs send the message that women are broken and need to be fixed in order to fit into corporate America or the culture the organizational hierarchy has designed for them. In nearly all instances, businesswomen feel they have worked ten times harder than their male counterparts to move up the organizational ladder. This is especially true for women of color.

Ninety-six percent of the 1,000 women we surveyed say that they have worked to fit the corporate mold. They also say they have masked their full voice and truly who they are to do so.[16] Participants tells us that they desperately want to be their authentic selves at work but feel they cannot do so for fear they will not be accepted and will consequently suffer from microaggressions. Ninety-nine percent of these 1,000 women in higher management positions—85 percent of whom were women of color—say that they have never felt they could be fully true to themselves at work without suffering negative repercussions.[17]

The top three leadership/professional struggles (especially for women of color) were:

1. Navigating a hierarchical paternalistic institution with leadership that lacked transparency (regardless of industry). Ninety-eight percent of the 1,000 women surveyed reported this as one of their top three greatest career and professional challenges.
2. Self-doubt/lack of confidence and/or imposter syndrome. Ninety-seven percent of the 1,000 women surveyed reported this as one of the top three greatest career and professional challenges. They say they often question themselves—asking, *Am I qualified enough? Can I do this?*—even though they have the credentials, experience, and success.
3. Lack of career/life balance, emotional exhaustion, and concerns about personal well-being. Ninety-five percent of the 1,000

women surveyed reported this as one of the top three greatest career and professional challenges.[18]

As our survey shows, women leaders are navigating masculine institutions with no transparency. And it is very hard to navigate because everything is so ambiguous. Ambiguity inevitably causes confusion and results in a lack of confidence.

A professional women's career growth and her impact in her organization is one of surviving or thriving. If corporations want women professionals to merely survive in their organization, they provide only basic survival requirements—food, air, water. But if corporations want women leaders—and their corporations—to thrive, then they need to provide the optimal environment including but not limited to: a fair compensation package inclusive of salary, health insurance, retirement plans, paid time off, bonuses, stock options, and other perks like flexible working hours or tuition reimbursement.[19] Corporations need to incorporate a culture that helps women thrive in a safe psychological and physical space. We strive to provide this at our institute.

Corporations need to incorporate a culture that helps women thrive in a safe psychological and physical space.

Our research also shows that the self-doubt women leaders experience comes from the fact that women don't get promoted as often as men, even though they are doing extraordinary work.[20] The struggle to ascend the organizational ladder leads women to question themselves: *What am I doing wrong? Am I not good enough? What's wrong with me?*

Let me show you an example. While hosting a private reception in my home, I was having a conversation with a colleague, Kevin, who is a managing director at one of the leading banks in the world. During our conversation his phone rang, and he apologized and said that he needed to take the call. He invited me to join him outside so we could continue talking afterward.

I walked out with him as he answered the call. It was from his human resource business partner, an individual dedicated to helping executives hire and manage their teams. He was reaching out because Kevin had an executive-level employee, a woman, Vanessa, who had done extraordinary work for several years. She had been passed up for a promotion before, and Kevin wanted to promote her soon.

The human resource business partner, however, insisted that there were no spots available for her. "I'm sorry," he said. "There are only three slots available for managing directors, and they have all been taken."

Kevin was not happy with this answer. He said, "It's not fair. She deserves one of these slots. They are always taken by men and we, as an organization, need to promote these highly qualified, hard-working women."

The partner suggested what he viewed as an alternative solution. "How about we send her to an executive leadership program to thank her for all her hard work?" he asked.

Kevin ended the call, feeling horrible about what had transpired. He explained that the managing director positions had been claimed by three powerful men who were grooming three more powerful men to succeed them. No matter how equipped, amazing, or hardworking Vanessa was, she did not stand a chance. Kevin could not give her the promotion she deserved. "This happens all the time," he told me. "There are very few of these managing director positions, and they are usually slated for and taken by powerful men who were groomed by other powerful men. Whenever I try to go to the table and move up the women on my team—the slots are 'called for' already."

He went on to tell me that these positions have to be spoken for a year or two beforehand, so no matter how hard women work, the odds are against them.

In my experience, it is often better for women to leave their current organization in order to move to a higher level in another organization. It is easier to get promoted elsewhere. Unless women are working at an organization that is actively and strategically moving women up to senior leadership positions (this can be witnessed by observing how many women are currently in top leadership in the organization), I always advise women who have worked really hard for years with no promotion in their current organization to move to another organization. I also tell organizations that if they want to retain their talented women employees, they need to begin designing systems that promote women.

It is not surprising that women of color don't see many people like them in high-level positions of power. Women often report they do not feel they are being "seen" or "heard" at work. Immigrant women struggle with a lack of confidence at higher rates than American-born women.

Navigating patriarchal institutions with leadership that lacks transparency causes women to feel self-doubt, struggle with self-confidence, and experience imposter syndrome and emotional exhaustion. It is a toxic workplace culture that desperately needs a transparent overhaul as the first order of business.

> **Navigating patriarchal institutions with leadership that lacks transparency causes women to feel self-doubt, struggle with self-confidence, and experience imposter syndrome and emotional exhaustion. It is a toxic workplace culture that desperately needs a transparent overhaul as the first order of business.**

Ungracious behavior in corporate settings has affected me, even though I'm in the business of leadership development, personal journey, and transformation. When we first launched our leadership programs in 2013, we were just starting to transform the lives of women leaders who were in turn positively impacting their organizations. We were having so much impact. However, early on, certain companies did not know how to integrate what we had to offer into their current company culture. We were too progressive for them, so they stopped engaging with us. Of course, at the time, we didn't know why this was the case, especially because they were the ones who had reached out to us. This lack of transparency began to take a toll on my self-confidence.

I knew women were being transformed. Corporations, nonprofit organizations, colleges, and universities were attesting that their people were being positively transformed. So, when they stopped engaging with us, I started asking myself, *What is wrong with me? What is wrong with our program? Everyone knows about the transformational impact we've had on so many women. We have hundreds of alumni testimonials and a track record of results.* I just didn't understand what had happened, and I started asking myself the questions 99% of women ask themselves in the workplace.

However, I would not be passive. I kept pressing, asking these organizations to share with me why they were choosing other leadership programs over mine. I did not get any responses, even though I knew they weren't getting the results we were. No matter how much I asked, no one would explain it to me.

Thank God for the work I do because it is what helped me discover I was falling into the same mental cycle many women do in their organizational environments. I was able to identify that there was nothing wrong with me or our leadership program. I was doubting myself because of the very system I was helping women challenge and overcome. It was the system that had been designed to adhere to traditional leadership development training and keep out anything that was not aligned with that specific design.

For nearly three years, this affected my efforts, my ability to be innovative, and my well-being. I was unmotivated. I was uninspired. I hired coaches and tried to create new and improved sales models. But none of this mattered because I was not being true to myself. It was not what I was offering that didn't work or was the reason behind why I was being rejected. It was the fact that what I was offering didn't align with the patriarchal, oppressive systems that currently exist in many organizations.

I had to reframe my entire perspective and experience with my company. I decided I would only partner with corporations, academic institutions, government agencies, and nonprofit organizations that aligned with our organizational values of progression and well-being. I decided that I needed to go back to square one: Focus on helping women become the most important version of themselves, so that they can transform into a better leader at work, as well as a better mother, community member, and overall better human being.

Now, we only work with organizations that are truly interested in approaching women's development with a holistic perspective, which is what we do. In order to work with us, organizations have to genuinely have an interest in helping their talent become better leaders and employees, as well as better human beings. Every human being on this earth has an impact on humanity as a whole. Our institute has taken on the responsibility to ensure every woman who goes through our program graduates with a Graciously Assertive Mindset—a mindset that is meant to help them become more thoughtful and empathetic people and leaders.

We begin the process by helping our students get clarity regarding their values. They have to examine what is important to them and what they feel is their purpose. Often, when this self-reflection happens, these students come to realize that their personal values do not align with those of the organization where they currently work. When they come to this realization, they have to choose how to proceed. Some choose to stay and help the organization change its culture. Others develop a strategic exit plan so that they can move to an organization where they feel they can be true to their principles. Whatever these women choose to do, we support them, and we love them.

Many of these women have experienced what I call "death by a million microaggressions" because our women experience so much passive-aggressive behavior that kills their soul. We help bring them back to life. Our program has been described by alumni as everything they didn't know they needed.

It is crucial to understand that when women lack Graciously Assertive self-advocacy skills they can fall into the trap of tolerating ungracious behavior, which only perpetuates the cycle.

Facing the Challenges

Many women of color feel that they can't truly relate to their managers. Many women came to a crossroad after the pandemic, when they realized career satisfaction must come with personal fulfillment. But they didn't know how to get there. That's where our program came in.

Ninety-five percent of our 1,000 women we surveyed stated that community is missing in their professional life.[21] They say that they don't have like-minded career women with whom they feel safe enough to share their everyday struggles and challenges and have found it difficult to relate to the advice and direction proposed by leaders in their male-dominated work environments. They have a hard time, they continue to explain, to connect with managers whose experiences are very different than theirs. They feel that their background—whether it is their gender, education, or ethnicity—has failed. Our program remedies this ill by bringing together like-minded women in a safe space where they can be their true, vulnerable selves, share their stories, and have necessary conversations.

Our program remedies this ill by bringing together like-minded women in a safe space where they can be their true, vulnerable selves, share their stories, and have necessary conversations.

It is crucial, as women leaders, to remember that our experiences and disadvantages are a part of our strength and contribute to our resilience. Good leadership begins with first acknowledging our vulnerabilities. After all, our vulnerabilities, in many ways, connect us with our humanity and with other people. It's a superpower that helps us transform our communities and organizational culture.

It is crucial, as women leaders, to remember that our experiences and disadvantages are a part of our strength and contribute to our resilience.

Many women feel their experiences of being biracial, LGBQT+, or being different in some other way have not been valued or represented in their professional environments. This lack of representation makes it challenging to work in in professional environments that do not honor them or their experiences. Black women experience the greatest difficulties based on my research because many are erroneously and derogatorily labeled as "angry." It is this very reason why GACM is so effective for all women; after all, it allows us to self-advocate while simultaneously being kind and direct.

Our research shows that no matter if a woman of color is a Harvard graduate, an attorney, a medical doctor, or a scientist, she will still suffer from imposter syndrome and feel that she's not good enough. Imposter syndrome is prevalent because many businesswomen do not see enough women like themselves in high-level positions. They think to themselves, *If people like me are not in these high-level positions, then what makes me think I'm any different or good enough?*

The broken system and inequities within organizational structures are not often or openly spoken about in society, and so women feel alone in their doubt. It is crucial to talk about personal experiences involving racism, sexism, and other forms of discrimination because doing so destigmatizes them. That's why we have an open dialogue at my program, where women say they feel the chains falling off them. Many feel gaslit by the system, confessing that they felt the micro-aggressions they were experiencing were all in their head.

Yet, when we come together and share our stories, everyone says, "Oh, my gosh! I am not crazy. All these times I felt that people were being sexist and racist toward me, it was all real. It's not just in my head because twenty-nine other women in my group have experienced it too." These discussions ultimately validate our women, and validation is the key in our program. Women need to feel validated. Many organizations ignore women's needs and their experiences, but when women feel seen and heard, transformation becomes possible.

Women need to feel validated. Many organizations ignore women's needs and their experiences, but when women feel seen and heard, transformation becomes possible.

The Significance of Holding Space

One of the most effective ways of avoiding ungracious behaviors is by holding space for the perspective of others in meetings, contentions, and conversations. Graciously Assertive communication has its foundation in empathy and requires us to acknowledge, listen, and validate the people to whom we are speaking. When we empathize and listen, we are holding space for others to communicate their thoughts and feelings freely, truly, and without fear of judgment.

Holding space begins with seeking to understand the other person's perspective. It is always about genuinely empathizing, asking the other person what they think and how they feel. It requires that we hear the other person's perspective before we speak and insert our thoughts and feelings. So, before stating your points, your opinion, your view, always, always, always start with listening to the other person. Really take into account what they are seeking to communicate. Don't just hear. Listen. This helps you avoid ungracious behaviors, and it will always give you the advantage in any interaction.

Holding space for others provides others with emotional safety. This allows them to let their guard down and express themselves honestly and openly. When you are holding space for others, you are practicing what I call being "Confidently Humble": being confident in your ability to lead the safe space yet humble enough to understand that the space is fragile and you must protect it. By holding space, our self-importance and ego is sent off—at least temporarily—into the background. When we listen actively, we give the person(s) we are addressing our undivided attention, focus, and ultimately our respect. Acceptance and nonjudgment are also crucial elements of gracious behavior and holding space for others. By holding space for others at the beginning of our interactions, we open the door for enhanced communication, understanding, and collaborative solutions.

By holding space, our self-importance and ego is sent off—at least temporarily—into the background. When we listen actively, we give the person(s) we are addressing our undivided attention, focus, and ultimately our respect.

Spotlight: Okeatta Brown

Below I share an interview with a courageous Black woman leader who embodies the Graciously Assertive Leadership style. Discover how she pushed back against ungracious behaviors in the workplace—particularly racism and microaggressions—to become the powerhouse business leader she is today.

Okeatta Brown

Okeatta Brown is the managing director; chief DEI, culture, and philanthropy officer; Mitsubishi UFJ Financial Group, Inc (MUFG) Americas, and global cohead of diversity, equity, and inclusion. Her successful career spans 25 years in the financial services industry. As a leader, she strives to develop corporate goals and strategic direction and encourage synergy and collaboration to drive positive change in complex environments.

Okeatta's expertise is found in the analysis of needs and issues, building partnerships, and developing innovative solutions which reduce cost, mitigate risk, build brand identity, and deliver exceptional customer, team, and stakeholder experiences. Her responsibilities include oversight of the company's philanthropic initiatives and developing and implementing worldwide DEI strategies.

She holds an MBA from Montreat College as well as a bachelor of science from Johnson C. Smith University. She is a certified Human-Centered Design Practitioner. She has served on multiple nonprofit boards, as well as the UNCF Maya Angelou Women Who Lead Luncheon Committee. She has been featured in *Savoy* magazine's 2023 Most Influential Executives in Diversity & Inclusion, *CALIBR Global Leadership Network* magazine, and Who's Who in Black Charlotte *Pride Magazine*'s 51 Most Powerful Women.

In Her Own Words

Yasmin: Tell me how your life story has propelled you to become the leader you are today.

Okeatta: My life story is a trip and a journey. Growing up it was my mother, older brother, and me. My mother did her absolute best to raise us to be good people, work hard, and love one another. One experience that helped shape the leader I am today was moving to a new home almost every year. This meant I was attending a different school each year from kindergarten through 9th grade. Through this constant change, I learned agility, flexibility, and independence at a very early age. My mother is the reason I know how to survive and thrive. She would never just give me the answer but rather force me to think critically about the full spectrum of the decisions I needed to make. I lean into these core principles every day as a leader.

Yasmin: It is hard enough to find good friends in one school, but having to do it in different schools every year is tough. Did you keep any of the same friends when you transferred schools, or did you have to find new friends every year?

Okeatta: Well, I'm a total introvert. It wasn't that important for me to always be with a group of friends. That said, I did find new friends, meet new teachers, and get used to a completely new environment with each move.

Yasmin: You've turned what many would see as a disadvantage, moving to a new home and attending a new school almost every year, into character-building strengths. Share with us how you have continued to transform your challenging life experiences into leadership strengths.

Okeatta: From a professional perspective, at my previous employer, there were two major acquisitions, one in which we did the acquiring and one in which we were being acquired. The ability to understand change and not being fearful of it becomes, "Okay, we're part of a new company. How do I demonstrate my value in this company? What can I do very well? What are my weak spots? How do I present it all in a way to maintain my position as well as gain the opportunity to grow and learn and evolve in my career?" Understanding that change is inevitable and knowing how to navigate it will enable you to thrive and help others make progress in their careers.

For example, when I joined my current company, my manager onboarded me and let me know she had decided to pursue a different job opportunity the same week. Three months later, the company announced a divestiture, selling a sizable portion to a large regional bank. I asked myself, *How do I adjust and contribute to the forward strategy for this organization? What do I need to do to be successful? What does the company need? What am I losing? What am I gaining?* From there, I said, "Okay, this is what the new structure should be. This is how we need to exist in this space to impact change going forward." Always keeping my front foot going and understanding change is going to happen is crucial. I need to be prepared for it and to prepare my team as well.

Yasmin: Over time your mind unknowingly creates a checklist of what you need to do to survive, to thrive, to get through each year. You become good at predicting and planning for the unknown. You took the survival need to be agile in your childhood and applied it to the workforce and cultivated it as a superpower.

Okeatta: That's true, creating a mental list of what, when, where, why, how and how much became natural to me. It was always, "What's happening here and how do I navigate it?" I learned to innately do those things and did not fully appreciate at that time that it's not everyone's journey.

Yasmin: What has been the most difficult time or greatest challenge you have faced in your life? What did you learn from it, and how did it make you a better leader and a better human being?

Okeatta: One of the more difficult times I've faced in my life was learning how to go through and get through trauma. I learned that I am courageous, formidable, and relentless about protecting myself. This protection can manifest through setting boundaries both in my professional and personal life and/or investing in my health and wellness. I try to find moments throughout the day that just belong to me. The work I lead requires that I lead with courage every day. I am consistently challenging norms, perceptions, and bias (unconscious or otherwise). I can't do those things without

The work I lead requires that I lead with courage every day. I am consistently challenging norms, perceptions, and bias (unconscious or otherwise). I can't do those things without courage. Nor can I do those things without affording myself and others compassion, grace, and space to live, learn, and forgive.

courage. Nor can I do those things without affording myself and others compassion, grace, and space to live, learn, and forgive. Being an effective leader means I am balancing all of this at once while also driving positive impact. It makes me a better human being because to be human is to be perfectly imperfect. If I keep this perspective in the forefront, it's impossible to lead with judgment and allows me to meet people where they are to move us forward together.

Yasmin: Do you believe becoming a better human contributes to making you a stronger leader? And if so, why?

Okeatta: Yes, I believe becoming a better human enables you to be a stronger leader. Early in my career, I was very matter of fact in my thinking. I was focused on "Work is work, your life is your life. We're at work, so let's talk about work." I realized that this mindset didn't allow my colleagues to really know who I was, and it didn't allow me to know who they were.

A great example of the importance of relationships is an annual review I received early in my career. One of the comments read, "Okeatta doesn't know the business. It would be great for her to learn more."

I was surprised and thought, *I know the business. What is this about?* My critical thinking emerged. *What if this isn't about the business but rather they don't know me?* I became more intentional in building relationships. I started to go for coffee breaks and talk with coworkers, finding areas in which we could really connect. I started to communicate better with members of the team who gave me feedback, and my next review was stellar. I didn't change what I knew about the business; I changed the relationships.

Yasmin: How has it been for you climbing up the corporate ladder as a Black woman? I know we don't have all day, but . . .

Okeatta: Early in my career, I never wanted to attribute my success or lack thereof to my race or gender. And then, those nuanced, sometimes subtle and sometimes not-so-subtle scenarios began to present themselves. I realized that I needed to have a "war chest," if you will. I would obtain the necessary credentials to ensure a "lack thereof" would not be the reason I didn't get an opportunity. I would make sure I was raising my hand for assignments that would yield development, great exposure and impact. It got to the point that the leadership at the time lamented, "Okeatta doesn't need another stretch assignment, she's stretched." And yet, the goal post kept moving. Lateral moves were my saving grace. They afforded me the opportunity to learn and evolve my transferrable skills over time across functions and lines of business. They were small steps of advancement but nonetheless valuable. I am a firm believer that everything you go through prepares you for the next thing.

In my case the lateral moves I made taught me change management, project management, relationship management, people management, strategy development, leading through influence, community engagement, the business of philanthropy, etc. My journey was met with quite a few challenges where I was put in a position to advocate for myself, to address what I deemed to be adversarial at best, and racist at worst. The ability to lead with courage was present then and now.

Yasmin: You have been identified as a Graciously Assertive leader based on the 8 Pillars of Graciously Assertive Leadership I created. As a leader, which of the pillars do you identify with most and why?

Okeatta: I'm surrounded by colleagues who support me and my team in advancing the work we're leading. Gratitude is the one thing I will highlight, underscore, and bold.

Self-awareness comes by asking, "What could I be doing better? How am I showing up? What did I contribute to make this outcome what it is? How can I change for the better as I move forward?"

Social awareness and self-regulation I had to learn. My self-regulation, for example, the fact I don't cry at work, is my business, and I cannot stand in judgment of those who feel freer to emote.

Yasmin: You are a very gracious communicator and graciousness is a form of kindness. Do you believe your ability to be gracious stems from your mindset of living in gratitude?

Okeatta: Absolutely. Living in gratitude allows me to give back and lead with compassion, empathy, and understanding.

Yasmin: My book, *Graciously Assertive*, defines a Graciously Assertive leader as one who is direct and honest, yet empathetic of the feelings and needs of others. Do you feel you have always been a Graciously Assertive leader?

Okeatta: No. Learning to be a Graciously Assertive leader I believe evolves over time. In my early days, I was very matter of fact, very direct and far less compassionate or tolerant for anything other than the task at hand. Then I evolved to what one leader coined as reasonably assertive, which I attribute to still being focused on the objective but also leading with empathy and influence, to then being Graciously Assertive, which I attribute to actualizing my leadership. This occurred when I became more self-aware and emotionally regulated and began to afford grace and space to and for others. Through leadership and lateral moves, I learned to navigate and take what I could from each move, including various leadership styles. I had to learn what to keep and what to leave behind. As I navigated project management, change management, marketing, relationship management, supplier diversity, strategy development, and diverse segment marketing, I learned a great deal that contributed to where and who I am today.

Yasmin: You chose to see every situation, every challenge, as preparation for the next day. You chose to see them as gifts to prepare you for the next level. You are a successful leader, a good human, gracious and kind, an all-encompassing leader who is a powerful combination of feminine energy, kindness, compassion, and assertiveness. Yet earlier, you mentioned kindness was not always a leadership trait for you?

Okeatta: Life cultivated it for me. I chose kindness when I could have gone the opposite direction. When I look back through my career, I remember an instance when a group of women, some who looked like me and others who didn't, told me I wasn't advancing because of my hair which was in "locs" or the clothes I wore which were professional, conservative, feminine, and stylish. They claimed others focused on what I looked like rather than what I said. One woman even offered to take me to a retail store for professional women. I graciously declined. I didn't need anyone to dress me, nor did I need to hide who I was. It was a strange feeling having colleagues who were senior to me at the time tell me I needed to hide myself. I'll never forget that experience.

Yasmin: Why is being assertive, firm, and direct in your leadership style important?

Okeatta: Being assertive is one of the cornerstones of leadership. Can you imagine if women hadn't been assertive, hadn't been willing to be courageous and step into the spaces we were told we couldn't be in? It takes an extraordinary level of courage and assertiveness to be a visionary and a pioneer. You must be willing to fail and keep trying over and over again.

It takes an extraordinary level of courage and assertiveness to be a visionary and a pioneer.

Yasmin: Why is being gracious in your leadership style important?

Okeatta: We're all human beings. It's important to not lose sight of that. It doesn't cost me anything to be kind. However, the inverse, depending on the circumstances, could cost me and/or the organization a great deal.

Yasmin: Do you believe your Graciously Assertive leadership style has helped you be a more effective communicator and leader?

Okeatta:. Yes. I started from a very different perspective. I have the proverbial tape playing in my head daily to help remind me to choose my words carefully so that I am effectively and graciously communicating with others. Having been on the other side and dealing with former leaders who demeaned me, shut me down, pulled my projects or took credit for my work, I know I don't want to be that kind of leader.

Yasmin: In terms of organizational leadership, how do you deal with failure?

Okeatta: Failure is learning. You can absolutely fail, but it's what you do with that failure that matters. Failure pushes you toward excellence if you let it. I don't look at a situation and say, "I failed." I acknowledge that whatever the attempt, it didn't work as I expected. Then I consider what I could have done differently or better. Who were my stakeholders, and what were their roles? Which stakeholders should have been at the table and weren't?—and so forth. Asking these questions allows me to point out where I may have missed an opportunity and try again.

Failure is learning. You can absolutely fail, but it's what you do with that failure that matters.

Yasmin: What happens when you have laid out your plans with your team and, for whatever reason, your team has not been able to deliver? How do you regroup and re-inspire people to double their efforts and move forward?

Okeatta: That's an interesting question, and I don't believe there's only one answer. Each leader is different. In my observations, if a leader isn't delivering, I first acknowledge there's a disconnect and give space for courageous conversation and constructive feedback. I listen with intent while also affording grace to manage through the issue, which could range from a lack of understanding of the ask to a lack of capacity to deliver due to resource constraints, burnout, etc. We work together to address the issue with a plan of action and reset expectations accordingly.

Yasmin: What areas of your leadership style do you wish you could do better?

Okeatta Self-care and self-compassion. While I create the environment for my team to practice self-care, I don't practice it fully for myself. In other words, I deeply believe in the work I lead and the imperative of building an inclusive culture. But sometimes I get lost in this passion and have to find ways to pull myself out. I need to do a better job of balancing the two.

Yasmin: Who are the people you most admire when it comes to leadership and why do you admire them? What influence have these people had on you?

Okeatta: I admire the women past, present, and future who dare to dream, to challenge, to innovate, and to build. The women who led/lead with courage and fortitude. The women who say to themselves, *If it doesn't exist, I'll build it and/or If there's no path for me, I'll blaze one*. These are the women I admire most and the shoulders on which I stand. I take the same approach professionally and personally. I tend not to stay in the confines of what is but rather build toward what could be. One great example of an extraordinary leader is Ethel Hedgeman Lyle, the visionary behind Alpha Kappa Alpha Sorority Incorporated, which is the first Black female sorority created on the campus of Howard University in 1908.

I admire the women past, present, and future who dare to dream, to challenge, to innovate, and to build.

Yasmin: What is the ultimate goal for you, the legacy you want to leave?

Okeatta: I'm going to spend the next several years building and creating a space to impact change. I don't want to have the same conversation around diversity, equity, and inclusion year after year but rather to leave the legacy of intentional inclusion.

Yasmin: Is there anything else you would like to share with the readers?

Okeatta: Being Graciously Assertive should be a movement you aspire to and live in daily.

CHAPTER EIGHT

TRANSFORMATION AND CULTIVATION OF A GRACIOUSLY ASSERTIVE MINDSET

Cultivating a Graciously Assertive Mindset brings about a transformation that could only be possible with the unique combination of graciousness and empathy with assertiveness and confidence. The results of adopting a Graciously Assertive Mindset are unexpected, highly effective, and powerful; the mindset allows us to navigate challenges seamlessly, overcome obstacles, achieve goals, and be better humans. Let's take a look at the elements of the Graciously Assertive Mindset.

Abundance Mentality holds that there is plenty of success to go around. Opportunities for success are abundant and ready to be shared by all. An abundance mentality is the opposite of a scarcity mentality. This toxic mentality assumes that there is never enough to go around.

Those with an abundance mentality focus on what they have and always aim for win-win situations. An abundance mentality boosts confidence and encourages collaboration. In the Graciously Assertive Lifestyle, an abundance mentality helps us approach situations with confidence and not defensiveness, seeing others as collaborators seeking mutually beneficial outcomes in achieving goals. When we have an abundance mindset, we can be assertive and empathetic and have no need to see others as competition who need to be undermined in order for us to achieve success.

Growth Mentality finds its foundation in the belief that challenges and obstacles present opportunities to learn, grow, and evolve. A growth mentality aligns well with Graciously Assertive Living as it encourages resilience, empathy, and openness, as well as self-improvement and zero tolerance for judgment. When challenges come, those with a growth mindset focus on opportunities for improvement rather than feeling discouraged. With a growth mindset and Graciously Assertive Communication, we can adapt in any situation, setting healthy boundaries, communicating effectively, and opening the doors to development, opportunity, and success.

When challenges come, those with a growth mindset focus on opportunities for improvement rather than feeling discouraged.

Gratitude Mentality has its roots in appreciating all the positives in life, including the contributions of others. Gratitude is one of the Graciously Assertive Leadership Pillars and fosters empathy, understanding, acknowledgment, and respect. In the Graciously Assertive Mindset, gratitude helps us seek a win-win scenario in every interaction, conversation, and encounter. With a gratitude mentality, we are more likely to engage others by actively listening with empathy and respect. It also allows us to freely express gratitude for the contributions of others, encourages collaborative solutions, and fosters community. A gratitude mindset also encourages collaborative solutions.

A Graciously Assertive Mindset requires that we adopt a mentality of abundance, growth, and gratitude. It allows us to remain self-aware and socially aware and teaches us to set healthy boundaries, be gracious to others, and assert our needs to ensure communication, collaboration, and community. Cultivating Gracious Assertiveness helps us confidently advocate for ourselves while also valuing alternative viewpoints. The result is understanding, unity, and positive transformation which helps us to be better humans and better leaders who can lead confidently, adapt effectively, and spawn growth in our organizations.

Abundance Mentality and the Cultivation of a Graciously Assertive Mindset

An abundance mentality is inspirational, allowing us to see the world as a place filled with opportunities, abundant resources, and endless possibilities. It is the opposite of a scarcity mindset which sees the world as a place of only competition with limited opportunities, possibilities, and resources. Cultivating a Graciously Assertive Mindset requires that we allow the abundance mentality to guide us. It increases our self-confidence, assuring us of a world of limitless opportunities and imbues us with confidence. This mentality reminds us that challenges and obstacles can serve as opportunities and possibilities and guide us in new directions for even greater success.

Abundance mentality also decreases our fears of rejection and failure. With an abundance mentality, we can see setbacks not as obstacles but rather stepping stones toward the future. It assuages our doubts and fears, allowing us to find our voice and better express ourselves. This helps us on collaboration, not competition. With a new cooperative mindset and abundance mentality, we are able to express our needs effectively while being empathetic to the needs of others. Furthermore, gaining an abundance mentality leads us to a more powerful desire for learning and growth. It allows us to see a world of knowledge and opportunities as diverse perspectives evolve. We then experience growth because we can more effectively assert ourselves and encourage positive change.

When we face challenges and setbacks, our abundance mindset can help us harness our resilience. With enhanced resilience we can be firm in our positions and state our beliefs with both grace and empathy. The abundance mentality also helps increase our sense of gratitude for unlimited possibilities. Our sense of gratitude becomes infectious as we share our positive outlook with those around us. Knowing the world is filled with limitless opportunities allows us to be more empathetic to other viewpoints and express our own.

In essence, the abundance mentality aligns perfectly with Graciously Assertive Leadership, empowering us to step out in confidence, articulate our needs with understanding and empathy toward others, and establish boundaries. By embracing both, we grow in our respect for others and can better engage in collaborative solutions with confidence, empathy, and open-mindedness.

Here's an illustration of how an abundance mentality nurtures a Graciously Assertive Mindset.

Suppose you've been working in a very competitive environment. You've been successfully working on a big project and invested a lot of time and effort. Now, you feel you deserve recognition and a promotion. You are not alone; several of your colleagues have also accomplished much and hope for recognition and a promotion.

With the abundance mentality, you come to realize that there are multiple avenues for growth and success in the company. While you want the promotion, you understand it is only one of the opportunities available if you continue to work hard and contribute effectively. You are able to approach your supervisor to discuss your achievements and state your interest in the promotion with greater confidence but also with the knowledge that other opportunities will arise if you continue to evolve on your path. During your interaction with your supervisor, you are also able to share your respect for your colleagues who also deserve recognition. Your abundance mentality allows you a unique perspective and helps you not be threatened by their achievements but realize the collective collaborative strength of the team will open doors for everyone.

This knowledge increases your willingness to collaborate with others, which opens the door to more projects and more opportunities. Your abundance mentality as well as your Graciously Assertive Mindset also helps you accept the outcome of the promotion. If it goes to a coworker, you won't see it as a personal failure but as an opportunity to learn for the future, finding areas for improvement and professional growth. It also allows you to be supportive of your colleague's success and be open to honest feedback as part of your own success journey. Here, in this example, the abundance mentality and a Graciously Assertive Mindset helps you not only communicate better but also find a road to future success through opportunities for growth and achievement.

Growth Mentality and the Cultivation of a Graciously Assertive Mindset

Having a growth mentality allows us to enhance our ability to be empathetic while nurturing our own self-confidence. Like an abundance mentality, a growth mentality actively cultivates Graciously Assertive Leadership. Embracing a growth mentality helps us learn from our mistakes, as we allow obstacles and setbacks to teach us and help us evolve. Within the confines of the Graciously Assertive Mindset, every challenge becomes an opportunity to reflect, learn, understand, and improve. Embracing feedback helps us improve, learn from mistakes, develop empathy, and refine our approach as we move toward success.

Graciously Assertive Communication requires adaptability helps us to adjust our approach in diverse situations. A growth mentality is the perfect companion in doing so, allowing us to embrace a variety of perspectives with empathy and understanding. Growth mentality also helps us continually nurture positive efforts and harness our inner resilience to achieve our goals. Along with our Graciously Assertive Mindset, growth mentality helps us effectively combine assertiveness with understanding. Self-improvement fosters Graciously Assertive Communication and a growth mentality helps us cultivate understanding, acknowledgment, and communication.

Challenges are viewed as opportunities for development within the growth mentality and guide us to constructively collaborate without confrontation. Growth mentality enhances our resilience in adversity, helping us to embrace our Graciously Assertive Lifestyle to face and overcome challenges, different opinions, and various resistance to our ideas. Graciously Assertive Communication thrives on openness to new ideas and diverse points of view, encouraging us to seek fresh ideas, increasing our ability to engage in meaningful and respectful conversations.

A growth mentality nurtures our adaptability to change. As Graciously Assertive individuals, we can navigate changing situations while maintaining our boundaries and upholding our values. This mentality also extends outward to everyone with whom we interact, helping us to share our thoughts and opinions and foster a collaborative environment for growth and understanding.

The growth mentality works to serve as a catalyst in the development of a Graciously Assertive Mindset, helping us to communicate, lead, and live with graciousness and assertiveness in communication and collaboration with others.

Gratitude Mentality and the Cultivation of a Graciously Assertive Mindset

The final component, a gratitude mentality, enriches our Graciously Assertive Mindset with confidence, empathy, and understanding. A gratitude mentality works hand-in-hand with Graciously Assertive Leadership and Lifestyle. Gratitude serves as the foundation for a positive outlook. A grateful heart gives us the ability to assert ourselves with grace, respect, and empathy in all of our relationships, from work to family.

Gratitude encourages emotional balance, helping us manage our emotions effectively. Gratitude prevents negative outbursts that can damage our communication efforts and our collaboration with others. With a grateful heart, we can express our thoughts with kindness and consideration. Gratitude encourages us to focus on the positive aspects of any situation, radically shifting our perspective and minimizing potentially negative confrontations, allowing us to address issues and challenges positively and assert our ideas with grace.

Gratitude deepens our capacity for empathy and helps us recognize and appreciate the contributions of others. This is because it allows us to be attuned to the feelings, needs, emotions, and points of view of our team members. Gratitude decreases our defensiveness because a grateful heart protects us from feeling threatened or attacked in communication or collaborative settings. It enables us to empathize with differing opinions, assert ourselves with grace, and become receptive to constructive feedback.

Gratitude deepens our capacity for empathy and helps us recognize and appreciate the contributions of others. This is because it allows us to be attuned to the feelings, needs, emotions, and points of view of our team members.

Gratitude encourages relationships through mutual appreciation as we nurture respect and collaboration. Gratitude amplifies our ability to listen actively and empathetically.

We are more able to hear and understand the perspectives of others and, in turn, can respond graciously and assertively with insights and consideration.

Gratitude brings positivity to conflicts. When we express gratitude for our opportunities, we can address issues with understanding and approach conflicts collaboratively, seeking solutions rather than confrontations.

Gratitude enhances our authenticity, too. When we are grateful for others' contributions, we value their input, allowing us to be both assertive and respectful. Gratitude, therefore, cultivates self-assurance. As we acknowledge our strengths and boundless opportunities, we can assert our needs graciously and maintain healthy boundaries without disrespecting others.

Gratitude enhances our authenticity, too. When we are grateful for others' contributions, we value their input, allowing us to be both assertive and respectful.

A gratitude mentality encourages positivity, empathy, and emotional intelligence with the pillars of Graciously Assertive Leadership. It enables us to express our needs confidently while embracing the principles of respect, understanding, and collaboration. As we develop gratitude, we foster gracious assertiveness for growth, harmony, and communication.

Finding the Gift

By embracing a gratitude mindset, I was able to overcome life's great challenges and discover my transformative leadership philosophy. As I evolved, I learned to see life's many challenges, including those many would call tragedies and failures as invaluable gifts. The process and the perspective have been transformative to my personal growth—allowing me to be a better human. This, in turn, has led to my growth and development as a leader.

When we face situations beyond our control, many of us—if only for a brief moment—panic and lose our focus. As leaders, we need to come to the realization that these situations provide us with a unique opportunity to refine our focus and redefine our perspective though the process of self-transformation. My Graciously Assertive Leadership philosophy is grounded in the belief that life's challenges and hardships should never be in vain. As leaders, we need to search for meaning in every difficulty and then refocus to find the gift in the situation. Once found, the gift should be embraced.

Committing to this approach has helped me to cultivate a mindset of gratitude which then gives me a peace-filled and joyous foundation from which I can be a better human and a more effective leader. Our perspective is fundamental to our leadership. The meaning we give to the events which shape us defines our ability to lead. By learning to focus on the gift in every circumstance, I have found life presents a continual stream of opportunities which allows me to grow, evolve, and develop. I can now intentionally choose to have faith, be positive, have hope, embrace optimism, and develop resilience in my journey as a Graciously Assertive Leader. Gratitude guides me, feeding my soul, but more importantly allows me to lead and guide others with greater empathy. This ultimately inspires my team to do the same.

Discovering Strength amid Failures

What do we do when those who are supposed to shield us from hurt fail to do so? Most of us would admit that sometimes we crumble and fall. However, when this happens, we must channel our inner courage and find our strength—even if those failures are the fault of others or our own.

My journey began in a tumultuous family. In 1968, my parents emigrated from Quito, Ecuador, and Chihuahua, Mexico, driven by dreams of a better future for me and their other yet-to-be-born children. However, my father's abusive behavior hurt our home, creating fear and anger at every turn.

At only five years old, I confronted my mother, confused at my father's behavior. I asked, "Mommy, why is Daddy so mean to us? Why can't we do anything right? Why is he always mad at us?"

Resigned, she replied, "That's just the way things are, *mijita*."

I could not accept her answer. With the determined passion of a five-year-old, I made a powerful promise. "No, Mommy," I said, "when I grow up, I'm going to change the world. I will make it better for mommies and little girls."

By the time I was eight, I mustered the courage to ask my mother why she didn't leave my father. Her response said it all: "*Mijita*, I don't speak English, I haven't been to school, I don't have the skills needed to make a way for us. If I leave, we may end up on the streets, and you and your sisters will end up in the same situation. You deserve to have an education. You *need* to have an education. Your grandmother once told me if I was a good wife, everything would be okay, but she did not tell me at what cost.

Promise me this, *hijita*, don't be like me. Go to school, get your education, then you can get a job and thrive on your own."

My mother had thus revealed the great price she paid for societal expectations, though it was not until I was older that I understood all she had meant with those words. One thing I knew was that my mother wanted me to have a great education and not live in fear. And so, I was determined to do it. I promised myself I would be the most educated Latina ever. It was a promise I realized when I earned my doctoral degree.

Some might perceive my upbringing with my father and mother as a failure, but I view it as empowerment. Although my father was mentally unwell and did wrong things, he unknowingly gave me the gift of purpose. At the tender age of eight, I uncovered what would be the foundation for my calling—to empower and uplift women.

My mother's story, although marked by hardship, is also one of resilience. She is a beautiful woman with an immense heart. She taught me empathy and compassion, revealing her inner struggle to escape the horrors we endured. Her example taught me that strength is different for each person. She also instilled in me the profound value of education.

Every failure conceals a gift awaiting discovery. We should never feel ashamed of our past or the adversity we've faced. I, for one, am proud of my journey as a Latina survivor, grateful that my traumas and tragedies molded me into the leader I am today.

Every failure conceals a gift awaiting discovery. We should never feel ashamed of our past or the adversity we've faced.

Putting It All Together—The Cultivation and Transformation of a Graciously Assertiveness Lifestyle

A Graciously Assertive Mindset is composed of abundance, growth, and gratitude mentalities and encourages confident, adaptable, empathetic, and harmonious engagement and leadership, focusing on open communication, mutual respect, and collaborative relationships.

An abundance mentality brings about boundless opportunities and resources, fostering confidence, resilience, collaboration, openness to learning, and reduced fear of rejection. It aligns with Graciously Assertive Living, allowing genuine and empathetic expression of needs and acknowledgment of others' viewpoints and needs.

A growth mentality sets healthy boundaries and allows you to become aware of yourself and surroundings. It also promotes a zero tolerance for judgment and treats challenges and failures as opportunities for learning, development, and evolution. This is made possible through self-reflection, improvement, and Graciously Assertive Communication, which requires empathy, understanding, acknowledgment, and respect.

A gratitude mentality is the final foundational element of the Graciously Assertive Mindset and brings positivity and emotional balance for every opportunity. It allows for Graciously Assertive expression, which is rooted in kindness, grace, respect, and understanding, and leads to collaborative solutions and win-win situations. A gratitude mentality is fueled by honesty, authenticity, and self-assurance, and this allows for growth, collaboration, communication, and community.

CHAPTER NINE

OVERCOMING THE CHALLENGES TO GRACIOUSLY ASSERTIVE LIVING

In business, as in life, we often face all kinds of difficult challenges. However, a Graciously Assertive Lifestyle can help us overcome those challenges. Being a good leader in business—whether we are just starting out, working our way to the top, or already there—requires that we be moral, as well as firm and direct yet kind, respectful, and considerate of the feelings and needs of others.

We all know there are lots of leadership books with a variety of methodologies trying to transform the business world as we know it. The question is: Are they transforming the patriarchal business world for women leaders of all cultures? Now, before we get started on this next topic, let me make it very clear. I love, empower, and embrace all women. It doesn't matter to me if you are a woman who is Latina, Black, white, Asian, Native

I love, empower, and embrace all women. It doesn't matter to me if you are a woman who is Latina, Black, white, Asian, Native American, Indian, or any combination of all—I will love you, support you, and help you thrive.

American, Indian, or any combination of all—I will love you, support you, and help you thrive. The same goes for men. I am committed to the betterment of humanity everywhere—no matter where you are in the world. With that said, there are some societal structures and systems that are hurting women of color, and I certainly will not shy away from discussing them.

For example, Sheryl Sandberg's book, *Lean In: Women, Work, and the Will to Lead*, was written with great intentions. It sought to offer pragmatic advice for women to grow in their careers. However, it did not acknowledge women of color—a fact that the author did later admit—and primarily laid the responsibility at the feet of women rather than at the foundation of systemic barriers holding them back.[22] After all, 85 to 90 percent of women of color face ongoing microaggressions in the workplace culture.[23] Trying to make it a woman problem and not a systemic structural problem simply doesn't work. When women of color "lean in," they are faced with questions and comments like, "Who do you think you are?" or "You're lucky you have a job." Even former First Lady Michelle Obama said, "That whole 'so you can have it all.' Nope, not at the same time. . . . That's a lie. And it's not always enough to lean in, because that . . . doesn't work all the time."[24] In truth, for women of color, it is hard to fit in, belong, or feel accepted. We are often made to feel that we are lucky to have a job and are forced to grin and bear it.

One Black woman reading Sheryl Sandberg's interview in Black Enterprise magazine commented, "Reading Sheryl's interview took me back to my days on Bay Street in the financial industry and my battle to belong. Truth is I wasn't able to lean in because I was still trying to understand and survive the microaggressions, emotional tax, and internalized oppression I was battling in the workplace."[25] The majority of women of color deal with this every day and cannot do anything. It is only when they feel they belong—and when they achieve a sense of security and confidence—that they will be able to empower themselves, "lean in," and say, "Hey, I could take this risk."

It is only when they feel they belong—and when they achieve a sense of security and confidence—that they will be able to empower themselves, "lean in," and say, "Hey, I could take this risk."

Taking risks is precarious at best because systemic structural oppression makes it almost impossible to do. Sheryl Sandberg's efforts were well-intentioned, but I think many elements in the book could actually be a hurtful guide for Black and Brown women who try to use it.

Furthermore, structural issues that are said to be made for all women actually hurt Brown, Black, and other women of color who are trying to move up in the ranks. For instance, there is a women's leadership assessment that is offered to organizations around the world. Although there are many positive attributes to this assessment, one of the leadership competencies for women to develop is boldness. They need to learn to stand up, to share, to express themselves, and to say how they feel.

Unfortunately, this assessment does not take cultural context into consideration and assumes all women are being perceived equally at work. However, as many of us know, this assumption is wrong.

In the *Harvard Business Review* article "The 'Angry Black Woman' Stereotype at Work," we find that "the angry Black woman stereotype has penetrated many parts of American culture, including the workplace. This pervasive stereotype not only characterizes Black women as more hostile, aggressive, overbearing, illogical, ill-tempered and bitter, but it may also be holding them back from realizing their full potential in the workplace—and shaping their work experiences overall."[26] Imagine Black women blindly using this leadership assessment as their base without taking into consideration that cultivating their "boldness"—without first nurturing their graciousness—may feed into the "Angry Black Woman" stereotype. When we use this assessment in our leadership programs, we make sure to address the cultural context of the lessons taught.

Another popular leadership style that I teach Latinas who are moving up the ranks to manage appropriately is the servant leadership style. A servant leader is a leader who shares power, puts the needs of employees first, and helps people develop and perform to the highest level possible. Although it promotes many wonderful qualities in a woman leader, such as humility, selflessness, and empathy, practicing servant leadership can backfire due to historically stereotypical Latina roles.

Although it promotes many wonderful qualities in a woman leader, such as humility, selflessness, and empathy, practicing servant leadership can backfire due to historically stereotypical Latina roles.

I'll never forget when one of the most prestigious leadership professors in the country, who was a white man, was teaching a leadership segment on servant leadership in my program at USC. He was delivering incredible content to my students until he arrived at an example of how he had "leaned in" on the practice of servant leadership. He went on to share how even though he was a vice president of a company, he didn't hesitate to help a janitor, who was working with only one arm because his other one was in a sling, pick up trash. This professor hailed the janitor as a servant leader and a role model to all. Someone even took pictures of him while doing his job, he explained, and his organization proudly published them in their weekly newsletter.

This story, for many reasons, was completely out of touch, so I jumped in and said, "For women of color, things work differently." I went on to share the story of one of our alumni, Laura, a senior director who was set to move into a vice president role. She had been in conversations with her manager about a potential promotion, and her manager had shared with her that she was ready. He had been inviting her to senior executive meetings to expose her to her next level of leadership. On one occasion, she was in a boardroom with nine executive-level men. When the meeting was over, the men gathered, and Laura joined a conversation with one of them. During this conversation, Laura noticed the cleaning lady, Lupe, struggling to gather and carry all the dirty coffee mugs from the executive table to the kitchen. Laura, having been brought up as *servicial* ("helpful" in Spanish) in a traditional Latino family, decided to help Lupe gather the mugs from the table and take them to the kitchen.

Laura said, "It was strange how the men looked at me with a surprised face as I helped Lupe. Some even stalled their conversation." Afterward, everything changed for Laura. Her manager stopped having conversations with her about the vice president role. She addressed it with him, and he told her that in conversations with other executives, they had all agreed she was not ready, that she needed to work on her executive presence. However, before the incident when she helped Lupe, her boss and the executive team felt she was ready.

Apparently, by helping Lupe, Laura had played into the Latina "maid" stereotype—at least in the minds of the executives—and this caused an immediate shift in their perception of her. I'm sure these elements were all practices of unconscious biases on the part of the men, but the fact is that Laura's story is a real-life example of what women, especially women of color, face in organizational toxic cultures.

Everything I have said about the toxic workplace culture aligns with the inability of women of color to "lean in." Telling a Black woman to be bold without teaching her to be graciously bold/assertive is the worst mistake we can make for her. After all, it only makes her fall into the "angry Black woman" stereotype. It is more important to tell her—and this works for all women—to be *graciously* assertive. When she practices this communication method, she is much more likely to be heard and get ahead.

Other strategies and tactics made for women will ultimately hurt Black and Brown women because they don't take into account equity or the importance of having a sense of belonging. So, will these other methods transform business for women in general? Maybe on some level, but not completely, and they certainly have not transformed women of color who are all still struggling to fit in their companies. My program, which focuses on Graciously Assertive Leadership, is designed to help all women become better leaders but also better humans. Even those who struggle with being assertive can learn through our program how to be moral, kind, and direct leaders.

The Question of Diversity and Inclusivity

One of our Graciously Assertive Leadership and lifestyle programs is geared toward multiculturalism. We focus on the experience of multicultural women, provide a safe space to be free from microaggressions, and nurture and love them. There is no other program in the world of which I am aware that helps women deal with core issues, social inequities, racism, and sexism. Our program is founded in diversity and inclusivity.

On May 30, 2020, as the world protested the killing of Black Americans, systemic racism, and police violence, a WhatsApp message popped up in our multicultural women's executive leadership program cohort group chat that profoundly impacted me. It read, "I literally can't stop crying. My heart hurts. I don't know what to do with the pain I feel or what is happening in this country to people who look like me. I do not know what I need. I just feel I need to share." The message was from Michelle, one of our Black fellow program sisters.

Within seconds, the message thread was filled with words expressing deep pain from the Black women in our cohort, and more from non-Black cohort members, including Latinas, Asian women, white women, and women of mixed races and ethnicities. I immediately called a virtual emergency meeting to discuss how we, as a multicultural women's executive leadership program, could address this problem.

As we all gathered in the virtual Zoom meeting, I could never have anticipated what would happen next. As a Latina with immigrant parents, who was born and raised in America, I understood that racial inequities exist, as my family and I had endured racism over the years. However, in my mind, we had survived and prevailed. Never, ever, ever could I have imagined what I was about to experience. I started the Zoom session by telling everyone, "We are here to hold space to share and support."

Michelle, sobbing uncontrollably, spoke first. "I am a Black woman," she said, "who is tired of being afraid of others who don't see us as human. We are animals to them. It's exhausting trying to prove we are worthy of rights. I'm exhausted and in deep pain."

Cassandra, a fellow Black cohort sister, added, "I'm afraid to let my husband go running in our neighborhood. I go with him even when I'm exhausted."

As I watched and listened to my Black women students share their deep pain, I felt heartbroken. "This is no way to live," I shared. "I never fully understood the fear and pain our Black brothers and sisters endure every day in this country until today."

This institute is led by multicultural women leaders. On that day, I promised to use our voice and platform to help alleviate dread and pain and to change and support the path to healing. The crisis born of systemic racism demands action, and we need to create a more equitable society for every member of our community. We must be part of the solution. We must lead by example; after all, if we don't, who will? This Zoom meeting changed not only my professional outlook but also my life. It redefined for me what diversity truly needs to be in order for our nation to become the best version of itself.

We need to create a more equitable society for every member of our community. We must be part of the solution. We must lead by example; after all, if we don't, who will?

Before we go deeper into the importance of diversity, equity, and inclusion and the challenges which need to be overcome, let's delineate the terms so we are on the same page.

Diversity, Equity, and Inclusion (DEI) Terminology

<u>Inclusion</u> means people across varying identities are and feel valued, welcomed, respected, included, represented, and heard.[27] Even more, inclusion means these individuals feel they fully belong and can be authentic, contribute to the collective, and have a voice. Inclusion requires actively, persistently, and systematically engaging diversity and fostering equity and social justice across all aspects of the organization, including actively identifying and removing systemic and other barriers.

- *This definition captures the feelings a person develops in a context in which their own personal culture is not the default culture. In this case, a person must learn cross-cultural behaviors. To balance power and whose culture is centered, we employ intercultural practices because this highlights how inclusion is clearly linked to concepts of diversity and equity. Inclusion cannot exist without its sisters diversity and equity.*

Inclusion, according to the Intercultural Development Inventory (IDI), "occurs when people are working together effectively, and their cultural experiences and differences feel valued and engaged. The terms 'D&I' are used together because of the recognition that simply having diversity isn't enough; inclusion is also needed so people can bring their unique experiences, preferences, and strengths to the table without sacrificing or minimizing core aspects of their identity, background, or expertise."[28]

Inclusion, according to the Intercultural Development Inventory (IDI), "occurs when people are working together effectively, and their cultural experiences and differences feel valued and engaged."

- *Think of inclusion in terms of the climate and experiences in a given organizational environment. Is it stressful? Is it welcoming? The way inclusion shows up shapes a person's sense of belonging.*

Multiculturalism/Interculturalism denotes people who come from diverse cultural backgrounds and have been brought together into a new environment.[29] From a societal perspective, think about immigration/migration and the encounter of different cultures. The setting may have a dominant culture which can lead to challenges in inclusion and equity goals.

Implicit Bias (defined by the American Psychological Association), also known as implicit prejudice or implicit attitude, is a negative attitude of which one is not consciously aware against a specific social group.[30] Implicit bias is thought to be shaped by experience and based on learned associations between particular qualities and social categories, including race and/or gender. Individuals' perceptions and behaviors can be influenced by the implicit biases they hold, even if they are unaware they hold such biases. Implicit bias is an aspect of implicit social cognition, the phenomenon which states perceptions, attitudes, and stereotypes can operate prior to conscious intention or endorsement.

Socialization is the process through which people are taught to be proficient members of a society.[31] It describes the ways individuals come to understand societal norms and expectations, to accept society's beliefs, and to be aware of societal values. Socialization helps people learn to function successfully in their social worlds.

- *This is part of the unlearning/re-crafting work involved in my leadership program. Critically examining our unique socialization process and challenging longstanding "truths" which no longer need to be real. This concept, from a DEI perspective, is also linked to how society treats the body in which you exist—whether your physical attributes or the groups with whom you are deemed associated.*

Social Identity is an individual's sense of who they are based on the social group(s) to whom they belong.[32] Social identities allow individuals to have a sense of belonging.

Social Justice refers to creating a society (or community, organization, or campus) with an equitable distribution of resources and opportunities, where all people are safe (psychologically and physically), can meet their own needs, and can fulfill their potential.[33]

Psychological Safety holds that everyone can pitch risky ideas and challenge the status quo without retaliation or judgment.[34] Psychological safety means feeling safe to take interpersonal risks, to speak up, to disagree openly, to surface concerns without fear of negative repercussions or pressure to sugarcoat bad news.[35] Psychological safety nurtures an environment where people feel encouraged to share creative ideas without fear of personal judgment or stepping on toes.

Intersectionality, as defined by Dr. Tanya Golash-Boza, is rooted in understanding how white supremacy, patriarchy, and capitalism are three interlocking systems which create hierarchies (race, gender, class identities).[36] This definition is derived from Black Feminist Leadership in which:

- Patricial Hill Collins argues these three systems are interdependent and can't be understood without looking at all three.
- Gloria Jean Watkins, better known as bell hooks, states these systems of oppression are interlocking—classism, racism, and sexism—and work to keep women exploited.

- Kimberlé Crenshaw, who coined the term "intersectionality" in a 1991 article, states, "Intersectional framework is necessary to understand the experience of women of color who have survived domestic violence including the impact of race, the unique impact of gender and the unique impact of class. When one's body exists in an oppressed identity of these categories, the impacts on the quality of life are unique and profound."

The word intersectionality has been co-opted and thus, when used in its truest sense, it:

- Applies to everyone, and
- Exists as a theoretical framework for how systems of oppression impact certain identities. It's about how multiple systems of oppression shape all of us.

Sense of Belonging is the feeling of security and support in which there is a general feeling of acceptance, inclusion, and identity for a member of a certain group.[37] It is when an individual can bring their authentic self to work. When employees feel they don't belong at work, their performance and their personal lives suffer. Creating genuine feelings of belonging for all is a critical factor in improving engagement and performance. It also helps support business goals.

Factors supporting a sense of belonging include:

- ☐ **Cultural responsiveness:** the idea that every person brings unique cultural strengths to the work place.[38] Recognizing and nurturing those strengths not only encourages success but also promotes an open-minded, supportive environment celebrating cultural differences.

- ☐ **Self-Authorship:** according to Baxter Magolda (2001), this concept is "the internal capacity to define one's belief, identity, and social relations."[39]

- **Community Cultural Wealth (CCW):** defined by Dr. Tara Yosso, this is the unique and valuable forms of knowledge, skills, and abilities possessed by marginalized communities.[40] Contrary to deficit-based views, CCW emphasizes that these communities have their own rich forms of capital, unrecognized by dominant societal standards.
    - Six Types of CCW:
        - Aspirational Capital
        - Linguistic Capital
        - Familial Capital
        - Social Capital
        - Navigational Capital
        - Resistant Capital

By tapping into our Multicultural Women Executive Leadership Program, women with various forms of strength and capital are able to reframe what they think is a barrier into a strength. The likelihood of this transition is linked to how the reframe helps them achieve the success they seek.

With our terms defined clearly, let's dig deeper.

Diversity is more than just integration. It is a state of mind. Diversity exists to embrace differences and integrate them into the fabric of our organizational cultures and our lives. That Zoom meeting inspired me to make the organizational decision to change our company's mission statement to reflect an anti-racist stance. We have since committed to being anti-racist and anti-oppressive in all facets of business.

Diversity is more than just integration. It is a state of mind. Diversity exists to embrace differences and integrate them into the fabric of our organizational cultures and our lives.

Our new mission statement, as of that date, states, "The Dr. Yasmin Davidds Leadership Institute is a multi-ethnic, anti-racist organization whose mission is to mobilize the transformation of women leaders as influential change agents, inspiring and strengthening alignment between their organization's business initiatives and social responsibility participation." It still surprises me that most organizations have not done the same and pretend everything is okay. The fact is that racism exists, and unless we actively stand against it, nothing will change. Organizations that don't acknowledge this are pretending it doesn't exist, as if nothing is wrong. Many people don't want to put that they are anti-racist in their organization's mission statement because they don't want to make a political stance. Yet, how can we not get involved in something that involves the killing of our people? Stating that we are an anti-racist organization is a bold statement and acknowledges the existence of racism and our commitment to stand against it.

When our organization went from a Latina women's leadership program to a multicultural women's leadership program, one of my Black fellow sisters came to me and said, "Dr. Davidds, I just want to share with you that two of my fellow cohort sisters were speaking Spanish, and I didn't understand them and felt excluded."

My immediate response: "We're going to fix that right now." I headed right into the class and stated, "Ladies, I understand how proud many of us are of speaking our native language. However, it is important to understand if anyone speaks any language other than English here, it means someone else feels excluded. With that in mind, I'm instilling and adopting a policy as of today that everyone is more than welcome to speak another language on the condition that you repeat what you said in English. It is a requirement because we want to make sure everyone understands and feels included."

Everyone, of course, embraced it and immediately began doing it. Now, whether on Zoom or in person, we share the policy at the beginning of every cohort. If, for some reason or another, someone forgets to translate, our leadership team will catch it and offer a translation in our chat. We make sure we do everything we can to ensure both diversity and inclusion.

Let's go deeper now and further define inclusivity and belonging. For me, inclusivity and belonging go hand-in-hand. A sense of belonging is about being a part of something greater than oneself. It allows a person to feel accepted, valued, and included in a group. It's akin to feeling at home—a place where one can be their authentic self without fear of judgment or exclusion. A sense of belonging involves feeling recognized, accepted, and affirmed by others and inspires feelings of security and support.

A sense of belonging is about being a part of something greater than oneself. It allows a person to feel accepted, valued, and included in a group. It's akin to feeling at home—a place where one can be their authentic self without fear of judgment or exclusion.

Women of color often feel the opposite in organizational cultures. They rarely feel they belong, part of something greater than themselves, and valued, accepted, or included. They may be asked to change their appearance or the way they speak, and this makes them feel like an "other." They can't be their authentic self without fear of judgment or exclusion.

Inclusivity is a sense of belonging, of being accepted and valued. It is the feeling that we are loved and appreciated for who we are, for our thoughts, opinions, and contributions.

The Importance of Inclusivity and Holding Space

We inevitably encounter people from all walks of life in a business setting. At first, it may appear easy to discern who they are as we take note of their **social identities**, a person's sense of who they are based on their group membership(s), which can include race, gender, sexual orientation, religion, abilities, and more.[41] Yet, we do not truly understand *who* they are until we are in a meeting discussing priorities, negotiating projects, or advocating for promotions. In these settings, the subtleties of our cultural backgrounds and societal norms which shape our behaviors emerge, whether we have intentionally done the work to explicitly name and carefully select our values or not.

As multicultural women, others can see our work ethic, our support toward colleagues, our concern for the vibrancy of the business. However, when it comes to our needs, our goals, our desires, the context of our realities may go unseen, unsupported, unacknowledged in a business setting. Why? Because our day-to-day experiences and the experiences held by other women reveal to us time and time again that our access to success is mediated by structural forces of oppression. Who we are, our most personal truth, can and has been judged, the bodies we exist in are discriminated against, our brilliance and expertise downplayed, and so much more. There is a value-judgment imposed on diverse populations because we are different from the norm.

Intersectionality in Inclusion Work

The challenges and barriers we face, including but not limited to imposter syndrome, show that not enough thought or investment into the practice of inclusion has been given in the corporate world. For example, if I enter a business space with my intersectional identities—a woman of color from a low-income background—the odds of these social forces creating barriers to my success can be incredibly strong. Thus, it is up to an organization to intentionally examine its policies, practices, and procedures to identify differential outcomes and ask themselves the following questions:

- Why are there two to three times more men in high-level leadership positions than women?
- Why is the gender-pay gap in my company stubbornly wide?

Efforts like these, designed to promote Diversity, Equity, and Inclusion (DEI), can make a notable difference in the experiences of multicultural women. While we know the role DEI can play in our experiences, I caution women about solely leaving it to organizations to identify DEI strategies to help make corporate navigation for multicultural women more fair and just.

In my years of experience in developing multicultural women, I realize that it is of utmost priority to focus on our *agency*, that is, our very own power and ability to affect the future. What are we in control of as we navigate inequitable forces and an unequal playing field? The answer I offer is *ourselves*: who we are, what we are in control of, how we move in the world, how we behave, and how we treat others. I advocate for an active approach that is within our control, and that means tapping into our truths, as painful as they have been, to develop the new narrative that liberates us from the traumas of our lived experiences. I know this is not easy because it is a raw process. This reflective and re-emergence work combines both the intersecting social identities we hold as well as our humanity and the trials and tribulations we have experienced. This is the fundamental foundation to my leadership programs.

People require tailored conversations to process their experiences in a way that expands their sense of intrinsic strength. The learning experiences provided by my institute give the individual something like a "playground," a safe emotional and intellectual setting to explore the narratives they've been telling themselves. Through the journeys of other women, she is able to gain access to tools, tips, wisdom, and strategies to help her navigate this so-called playground, as the safe space ultimately serves as an incubation for the achievement of her future personal, career, and leadership goals.

Holding Space by Systematizing Inclusion

"Holding Space" for others begins with systematizing inclusion in teams, departments, and organizations. My passion began and remains grounded in helping multicultural women explore their lives to unlock their leadership potential and make their difference in the world. It is my end goal, but I know the process starts with moving through this emotional and intellectually intensive journey and continues as we create inclusive systems to guide the process.

Women come to my program with a sense of who they are, and they leave with an awareness of who they must become to achieve personal well-being and inner joy. Imagine the gap between these two versions, and then visualize it. To allow the transformation to take place, I create a carefully designed inclusive environment. In this environment, the magic convenes—my passion, our experienced advisors, research informing the learning within the leadership program, and the combined expertise of the cohort. As its steward, I've learned that growth happens when we nurture this environment, the incredible place where we "hold space" for one another.

In the busyness of our lives, it can be challenging to find time to pause and consider what our lives have become—how we spend time, how we take care of our bodies, the relationships we foster, and the goals we are striving to achieve. By the time women contemplate the program, they have an awareness that this go-go-go lifestyle has depleted them. They intuitively know they are unsatisfied but may not have the language or invitation to unravel why. Some may know how they've reached this point but have not been able to identify why they feel this deep, achy sense of dissatisfaction. Others come to the program overwhelmed with frustration and the pressures of dreams unfulfilled. Each of these scenarios needs an environment in which to unravel, untangle, and re-arrange itself in a manageable way. Whatever their point of entry into the program, the process of transformation soon becomes clear for all.

In the busyness of our lives, it can be challenging to find time to pause and consider what our lives have become—how we spend time, how we take care of our bodies, the relationships we foster, and the goals we are striving to achieve.

In the program, the journey of transformation begins from one of these three orientations:

1) What is the individual's readiness potential to put in the energy necessary—that is, their capacity for putting time on their schedule to be real not with both themselves and others who are on a similar journey? How strong is their desire to transform? How far along are they in this awareness journey?

2) How does the individual explain their openness to feedback and mirror-work? It is the type of reflection which goes way past the tip of the iceberg. It is the exploration, though possibly never before verbalized to another human being, that significantly informs how they move through their personal and professional lives.

3) What is the individual's orientation in being generous with their lived experiences to support the learning of other women? What wisdom or navigational stories can they share with vulnerability and transparency? This is particularly important because we all hold experiences that can powerfully resonate with others. To acknowledge all we go through in life elicits an awareness that sharing our stories is a practice to illuminate clarity for others, especially in ways we could never imagine.

Scanning for these three orientations, one defines the embarkation on the journey of transformation. It is the responsibility of the program to set the stage of an inclusive environment, a nonjudgmental space where our women can share the pain of their life stories, their crucibles. It is my protective duty to ensure we see each other without judgment, so my team and I structure the pathway to self-awareness with readings, exercises, fellowship calls (one-on-one meetings with fellow cohort members), and other relationship-building activities to help them become more comfortable with the challenges they are navigating. As we witness each other's truest self, participants, advisors, and I share affirmations, words of wisdom, and stories to bring healing to the pain and trauma they have experienced. We help them understand their past and future from a "both/and" position, allowing them to take ownership and love the parts of themselves which may have been filled with shame. The community and the culture we establish in the program is so unique because transformation is not rooted in book work. Yes, theory informs our practices, but to support the process of transformation, our participants must both feel and think about the work.

What exactly happens in this inclusive space? It's a series of invitations mixed with offerings. For example, our first invitation is to have our participants share their "crucibles," their life stories and adversities they've overcome along the way. Participants may at first be fearful, yet because of their awareness of our intent and goal—as well as the knowledge that this first invitation has the power to liberate them from considerable pain or angst—they accept it. They take a deep breath. They jot notes. They grab tissues. They speak. They exhale so much more than air. In this space, they are seen with their social identities—women, mothers, immigrants, etc.—as well as their professional identities—titles, roles, and responsibilities, workplace navigational challenges, and work-life integrated dreams and goals. As they humanize themselves and each other, we create a community of human beings, unadorned and genuine.

These women never forget their identities and life experiences, but they begin to exist with a fresh awareness of their identities and not narrowly defined by them. With the expansion of awareness in who they are, each participant starts to create an internal space of *self-authorship* (the internal capacity to define one's belief, identity, and social relations) in their hearts and discover who they are and a new sense of power and confidence. They release the shame and suppression of their real stories, and the dynamic exchange is the process of transformation. After three months of integration and a deep sense of community *cultural wealth* (the unique and valuable forms of knowledge, skills, and abilities possessed by marginalized communities), each participant is much closer to becoming the version of themselves they seek while intricately experiencing a self of belonging.

There are those who believe they cannot replicate this type of space in the workplace, where urgency or transactional processes underlie workplace cultures. However, I firmly believe that, with an ethos of love, any one of us can hold space for others. To create an environment of inclusion and holding space, consider the following:

- Plan for a meeting of individuals from diverse backgrounds. Frame and ground the meeting by honoring the diversity in the room. Set the community norms clearly with space to allow the audience to seek any clarifications they need.

- Practice radical curiosity as individuals share their experiences. Practice active listening and echo back to ensure you are hearing their stories correctly.

- Amp up awareness of any negative orientations toward conflict, whether they are reactionary responses to conflict or orientations toward conflict mediation or resolution.

- Study and uplift the work of diversity, equity, and inclusion at the organizational level—by, for example, learning and implementing policies to help people of different backgrounds overcome the unique barriers they have face in the workplace—so staff and leadership become culturally responsive. It can come in the form of affinity groups, hiring and retention practices, cultural and heritage celebrations, or implicit bias education.

- Balance out loud voices and quiet ones. As a facilitator, recognize the individuals who haven't spoken or participated. Do not assume it is because they are unengaged. Make the invitation to express what may be on their mind in the moment.

- Last but not least, courageously explore your own story as a tool to help build compassion with others. "Remember: despite how open, peaceful and loving you attempt to be, people can only meet you, as deeply as they've met themselves."—Matt Kahn

As leaders, the skills which can help us create this space include practicing the six principles for Holding Space: Emotional Safety, Radical Humility, Active Listening, Acceptance, Nonjudgment, and Compassion.

A Community of Multicultural Women

The key component of my approach to a community of multicultural women is **cultural awareness** (the understanding of the differences between oneself and people from other countries or backgrounds, especially differences in attitudes and values).[42] Every woman is subject to cultural expectations that have impacted them, not only in life but in the workplace. Sometimes, the behaviors, mindsets, and considerations they develop can impact them in a negative way because the existing, though unconscious, cultural norms may not match behavioral norms expected in the workplace.

The key component of my approach to a community of multicultural women is cultural awareness (the understanding of the differences between oneself and people from other countries or other backgrounds, especially differences in attitudes and values).

One example that comes up time and time again is the rationale behind our (multicultural women) approach in leading teams and the actual effect and impact we are having. When we realize we are not as impactful as we hoped, we often start to develop a lack of confidence, second guess ourselves, stop asking for raises or promotions even when we know we are stellar employees and are receiving exceptional reviews. This demonstrates the fact that while we have gained understanding that cultural expectations and in our lives, are deeply entrenched because of our upbringing, we are still operating from an unconscious manner. We, then, allow cultural barriers to interfere, not because they are wrong but because we haven't had the opportunity to understand the difference between our culture and the culture expected in a business setting. Once these unconscious self-sabotaging behaviors (self-sabotaging because they aren't effectively moving us toward success) become conscious, we have the power to transform ourselves by adopting self-empowering behavior.

I help diverse women reframe former cultural mindsets and create new mindsets that facilitate empowerment and find their voice to help them thrive. Yes, *thrive*, despite all the systemic and gender imparities that exist in the workplace.

Throughout over 20 years of serving multicultural women and strategically recruiting diverse cohorts, I realize that even though we have different cultures, social norms, workplace practices, and backgrounds, there is something we all share: *the desire to be seen for who we are as we are.* Working with multicultural women is unique because when we come together, we are able to explore both our differences and our commonalities. As women, we all have experiences with patriarchy and social norms regarding how women *should* behave—that is, quiet, selfless, etc. Yet, as we begin to hear each other's stories, we gain an additional tool in our skill set—the mirror of self-reflection.

Intersectionality

All women hold various intersecting identities. How we each experience gender bias, racial discrimination, and income backgrounds in the workplace all dynamically interact with how we are afforded opportunities for success. For some of my students, gender identity seems to be the strongest influence on how they shape their world. For others, racial identity is strongest. Yet, for the majority, understanding the dynamic interplay of two or more of these identities in their current reality is key. The experience of a white, queer woman from a middle-class family is different from an Asian, differently abled woman from a working-class, immigrant background. A Black immigrant woman whose parents went to graduate school will have a different experience from a Central American Latina who went through the foster care system and started her college journey at their local community college. Ultimately, my leadership work starts with each woman identifying their own intersectionality, understanding how gender and cultural norms have benefited and/or harmed them in the workforce.

All women hold various intersecting identities. How we each experience gender bias, racial discrimination, and income backgrounds in the workplace all dynamically interact with how we are afforded opportunities for success.

Psychological Safety

The wide variations of experiences and backgrounds reflect the incredible richness of the women who come to the program. So, how do individuals with such different personal backgrounds and professional experiences find common ground?

Part of the reason is the systematically designed, psychologically safe space we hold for them to meet and see one another with loving compassion. Every single woman of color feels seen and heard, and they don't have to be ashamed of their experiences, especially those who they feel they stand. As a group, we process feelings of shame or perspectives that place us as disempowered victims in our story and feel the relief as it is received without judgment or criticism. We normalize the traumas we've been through, not to "approve" them, but to acknowledge them as part of our histories. The women also gain a sense of solidarity as they realize other women share their story or have gone through things they couldn't imagine. This allows the women to develop unshakable sense of respect and camaraderie.

Strong Sense of Belonging

As the women connect with one another, they gain a strong sense of belonging. This helps them feel warmly welcomed, accepted, and free to exist fully as themselves. There is no code switching or likeability politics; there is just you, in your beautiful humanity, and the expertise you bring into the space. In a business setting, you have to create the environment—a safe space—that allows individuals to feel respected, seen, and heard. Doing so requires an awareness of the nuanced difference between the terms diversity, equity, and inclusion.

In a business setting, you have to create the environment—a safe space—that allows individuals to feel respected, seen, and heard. Doing so requires an awareness of the nuanced difference between the terms diversity, equity, and inclusion.

Implicit Biases

Diversity lets us see that everyone's lives have been undeniably shaped by the communities with which they identify, communities that either are being subject to discrimination and systemic exclusion or benefit from social privilege, such an upper- or middle-class background. Equity allows us to understand that to help unique individuals reach their goals, we need conversations, resources, exercises, and relational support that are tailored to their needs. The key difference between equality and equity demonstrates that while I may be able to give everyone in my programs access to our seminal text and training, it is not always enough. After all, because of their unique lived experiences, what they ultimately need to transform must be tailored to the situations they navigate. Thus, when I teach my students the strategic options and tools needed to navigate the corporate political landscape and thrive, they learn to take the tools and make them their own. This helps them ultimately move away from deficit thinking and challenge the ideas which make them feel something is "wrong" with them.

Multiculturalism

For example, as professional leaders we all need tools to learn negotiation, skills to be assertive, and strategies to deal with microaggressions, and more. However, how those show up for each of us will be different. For instance, if a woman comes from a business family, to what extent will she need negotiation skills? If a woman comes from a culture where direct communication is practiced, to what extent will she need skills to be assertive? These may not be the specific areas of support needed but, because of the breadth of topics covered, women learn to identify what they need, govern who they are, and take power over what is within their control, even if they are still afraid to exercise their newfound power. Therefore, while the leadership principles are the same, women find their version of leadership to beautifully complement their values, voice, and passion.

Through the relationships they build within their cohort and the leadership development they receive, my students are ready to assert their power in the industries in which they work. In this global society, a leader who is a multicultural woman, grounded in her truth, and equipped with the skills that allow her to see her staff, colleagues, or superiors as human beings, is an incredible asset.

How We Teach It?

Many of you may be wondering, *Shouldn't people know all this?* Others may be asking themselves, *If people don't know this, how can you teach it?* Keep in mind, not everyone needs to learn every part; in fact, most of us know some of it, and what we don't know, we can learn.

Here's how we teach it. When women come to our Multicultural Women Executive Leadership Program, they are taught to understand what inclusivity and belonging feel like. We lead them to greater understanding of what inclusivity means through a guided visualization exercise.

It goes something like this:

- Close your eyes and imagine the first day of a brand-new job.
- You're outside the building. You're so excited to go inside because you've been waiting for this job.

- You walk through the big glass doors and have a feeling of belonging. What is happening? What is going on? It feels so right and so good. It feels like you've come home.
- Look at the walls, at the people. Is there art on the walls? Are the people smiling at you? What are they saying to make you feel like you belong?
- You're walking through the halls. What is happening to make you feel so at home?

We take them through the process, and then have them open their eyes and document their answers. What did people say to them that made them feel included? What was the tone with which people addressed them? What behaviors did they practice to make them feel included? The goal is to help my students have a visceral experience of what it feels to be included and what it feels to belong.

Afterward, I tell them, "Whatever made you feel like you belonged are behaviors you must practice to help others feel like they belong, even the white executive men you may feel intimidated by. You must practice these behaviors of belonging with them as well." It all goes back to my philosophy: Don't ask for anything you're not willing to offer. Do unto others first whatever it is you want to be done unto you.

It all goes back to my philosophy: Don't ask for anything you're not willing to offer. Do unto others first whatever it is you want to be done unto you.

If we want others on our team to feel a sense of belonging, we need to become more inclusive. Inclusion is powerful. Every organization can become stronger, healthier, and more productive if it integrates it into their values. After all, whatever it is we want to see in our world and in our life, we have to become it first.

My philosophy is that you must not ask for anything you're not willing to offer because, honestly, unless you're willing to offer it, you don't deserve it. You only deserve what you're willing to offer to the world. Don't ask the world to give you something you're not willing to give back. Don't ask your job or company to make you feel like you belong if you're not making others feel like they belong.

We need to actively be inclusive and make a plan to welcome others. Ask yourself: *What will I do to help others feel like they belong? What behaviors will I practice for the next seven days? When and where will I do it? How will I continue to make sure I practice it? What will I say? What will be the tone that I use?* We have to plan it out, write it down, and do it. We have to learn to be what we want. We can't merely teach on inclusion and belonging; we need to integrate it into our values and lifestyle and manifest these principles in our own lives.

CHAPTER TEN

BETTER HUMANS MAKE BETTER LEADERS

The premise behind this book, *Graciously Assertive: How Becoming a Better Human Being Makes You a Better Leader*, should now be clear: Better humans make better leaders, and better leaders make the world a better place for us all. Honestly, I didn't set out to prove that becoming a better human makes you a better leader. However, over twenty years of working deeply with women in leadership and going to the depths of introspection have proven to me that improving who you are as a person absolutely makes you a more effective leader.

You've seen here how I help my clients and students become better humans. It is through a process of deep self-reflection that my students are able to achieve a better understanding of their life experiences that have shaped them into the human beings they are today. However, what got them to this point in life—the trauma and the tragedies—will not get them to the next level of leadership. The psychological behavior patterns of their past need to be unlearned so that they can achieve the next level of success at work, at home, in intimate personal relationships, and in their well-being.

For example, one of my clients, Vanessa, was an upcoming director of human resources at a leading global artificial intelligence company. She became the first-ever Head of Global Diversity, Inclusion, and Belonging in the organization—a position that was created following the George Floyd murder. Vanessa had been successful in her work and what she had accomplished. She had risen to a director, having successfully worked her way to the top.

Now, in this new position, she had to step up in a completely new way, to reach across the entire organization and build strong alliances with global leaders throughout the different sectors of the company. All her life she had been hyperfocused on her work performance, having built an emotional armor that didn't allow anything or anyone to distract her from reaching her career objectives. However, in this new elevated role, she needed an entirely new set of emotional intelligence skills. After all, she needed to establish deep connections with global leaders and influence high-ranking members across departments. But how could she establish emotional bonds when she had hardened her exterior to protect herself? She had always been wary of trusting others.

When she was young, Vanessa believed she could make it in life without placing her trust in others. Why? She had been abused as a girl. And so, she shut down her emotions and decided that she didn't need any help. She had gotten to where she was by disconnecting herself from her emotions, even from her husband and child. She was aware of her emotional disconnect, but also knew that it allowed her to focus on getting the results she needed and achieve success—at least up to this point.

However, this position was very personal to her. Initially, the job title did not include the word "Belonging." In fact, the position she applied to was "Global Head of Diversity and Inclusion." But then, during her interview for the role, she purposely added *Belonging* to the end of it. Why did she do this? Well, Vanessa had realized that she had pushed through her life not trusting people, and this made her feel as if she never belonged anywhere. While her emotional armor had guarded her, shielding her from vulnerability, it had also kept her from forming close connections. And so, even in a room full of people, she always felt alone. In fact, she always felt alone—in her marriage, with her friends, and even with her child. While her armor had protected her from anyone ever hurting her again, it also kept out the love and connection she desperately craved.

In Vanessa's mind, this new position was an opportunity to create a sense of belonging for the company's employees—a sense of belonging that she had never experienced herself. It was very personal to her. And so, when offered the position as Global Head of Diversity and Inclusion, she negotiated to add the word "Belonging" to the title. The company granted her request, and she became the first Global Head of Diversity, Inclusion, and Belonging for a leading global artificial intelligence company.

Vanessa was someone I had worked with as an executive coach many years ago. Now that she had been appointed to her new position, she returned to me and said, "I need a playbook for this position. I need to know how to elevate the game at my company. I need to know how to create a sense of belonging here. Will you help me? Will you guide me? Will you be my executive coach again?

I answered, "Absolutely," and we began working together again.

Vanessa's commitment to excellence was intense and clear, but her need to succeed was driven by external validation.

Her success equaled her self-worth. Her success gave her significance. Her success at work made her feel she was a worthy individual and human being. Since no one can control whether they will succeed at the next level, Vanessa lived continually in fear and anxiety.

Anxiety and fear-driven ambition caused her a lot of physical issues, including severe, chronic gastrointestinal issues that had sent her to the hospital again and again throughout her adult life. Her emotional armor had caused a disconnect with her son, her husband, her colleagues, and her very limited number of friends.

Even so, when she came to me, she desperately wanted a plan to succeed. She wanted to create a place where she could feel she belonged. As we began working together on a plan for diversity, equity, and belonging, she came to me and said, "I'm really frustrated. I realize that no matter what I put on the table, my company doesn't seem focused on a sense of belonging. I offer an idea, and they reject each one even after I explain. I know our employees need to see people like themselves—people of color—to feel as though they belong. But the company doesn't want to put any numbers, deliverables, pressure, or sense of responsibility on anyone. So, I don't know how they want me to meet these goals of diversification, inclusion, and belonging."

No matter how much she pushed—or how many plans she presented or strategic goals, activities, and action she delivered—the company pushed back. She started questioning herself and coming to me, asking, "What's wrong with me? Everything I put on the table, they reject. What am I missing here?"

She felt like she was losing it. Distraught, she added, "I just don't understand."

Vanessa had reached success by being strategic. Now, all of a sudden, she was doing what she had always done, putting recommendations on the table, and they were all being rejected. She could not understand what her company was saying or what they wanted her to do.

The truth was she wasn't missing the mark or doing anything wrong. There was just a misalignment in values between her and her organization. After all, she had never worked on anything that was value-driven. For the first time in her life, she was seeking a sense of belonging that she had always been longing for.

Vanessa realized, over time, that the organization was not truly invested in helping employees feel they belonged. They were truly invested in looking as if they were doing the right thing.

Therefore, everything was a farce—it was not real. Vanessa was heartbroken, angry, and full of anxiety. She could not help employees or external customers build trust in the company under pretense. But what could she do? Her anxiety worsened, as did her physical ailments. She was in the middle of a professional crucible, what many would call a crisis.

As we worked together, she confessed, "I don't know what to do. I can't pretend any more. I'm tired of pretending. I'm tired of not feeling as though I'm truly connecting to creating a sense of belonging. Something has awakened in my heart and soul, and I cannot put it to sleep again. It has allowed me to begin opening up and removing my armor bit by bit. I've begun tapping into myself, my sense of belonging. I could have helped thousands of employees feel like they belong, and now that feeling has been ripped away from me because it has all been a pretense. I don't know what to do."

I answered, "You have to learn to lead yourself first."

The first step she had to take before she could ever help others belong or lead a company in a DEI initiative was lead *herself.* She had to be clear on who she was as a leader, who she wanted to be as a leader, and come up with a very loose road map on how to get there.

She wanted a step-by-step plan. She wanted me to tell her what to do—step one, step two, step three, etc. She asked, "How do I lead myself?"

It is difficult for people to do what needs to be done and to lead themselves first because we, as human beings, are wired to immediately look outside ourselves for a plan. We are not taught to look within ourselves, to lead ourselves first. This is an issue because it is only through an introspective journey of self-leadership that we can ever truly fulfill organizational goals and become the leader we are meant to be. We must sit down and conduct a deep self-examination of who we are, why we are who we are, how we have become this way, and what we need to do to become the best version of ourselves, the best humans, and therefore the best leaders in our organizations.

We must sit down and conduct a deep self-examination of who we are, why we are who we are, how we have become this way, and what we need to do to become the best version of ourselves, the best humans, and therefore the best leaders in our organizations.

Vanessa asked again, "Can you give me a plan to follow to get through this?"

I told her, "You have to get clear on who you are as a person, and who you want to be as a leader for this company, as well as in your life. In other words, it's time to get vulnerable and do a deep self-examination."

She answered, "Just give me the steps. Give me the plan to get vulnerable. I'll do it. One, two, three!"

But I had to be honest with her. "There is no plan," I said. "It is a process you must go through. You may think you're ready, but you'll have to go through the process with my team, and only if you're truly ready."

You can accomplish deep introspection in one-on-one coaching, which is what I do with my executive coaching clients. But if you really want to go to the next level with a sense of love and support and understanding, you need to do it with community. This is the best way to accomplish your goals. I can only reach so many with one-on-one coaching, but when I bring my students together and guide them through the transformation of self-introspection, they are able to grow and thrive.

However, in order to be accepted into our leadership program, individuals must be ready to be vulnerable. They can't just talk about it. They need to truly express themselves. However, most people don't know how to be vulnerable or even what true vulnerability looks like.

This was the case with Vanessa. She went through the interview process with our leadership team who asked her about vulnerability. When the interview was over, she called me and said, "I am so excited. The interview was flawless. I connected with the interviewers. I became vulnerable. It was wonderful."

I was so thrilled for her. This was a necessary next step in Vanessa's journey, and it would help her build community and transform as a person and leader. However, when I spoke to my leadership team, the interview panel gave me bad news. "We're sorry," they said, "but she did not pass the interview. She cannot be accepted into the leadership program because, while she talked about vulnerability, she did not exhibit it."

"What do you mean?" I asked.

"She talked about her son being autistic," they said, "and the struggles she went through with him. She said she needed to be vulnerable in order to accept her son's autism because it was difficult for her, but she did not share about how it made her feel. She did not share what it did to her heart and soul. She was not vulnerable but only talked about vulnerability."

Vanessa did not know the difference. She thought talking about vulnerability was vulnerability, and the interview panel did not feel they connected with her. They felt she was superficial.

I went back to Vanessa and said, "I'm sorry but the interview team did not feel you were vulnerable."

She was perplexed. "What are you talking about?" she asked. "I was super vulnerable. I don't understand."

I answered, "Okay, it's time that you meet with the leadership team, and they will share with you what they witnessed to help you better understand."

Vanessa sat down with members of the interview panel who explained what vulnerability was, and she finally said, "Oh, my gosh! I need to talk about how it made me feel? I need to talk about how seeing him struggle caused my heart to ache and my stomach to turn? About how tears welled up in my eyes in my darkest moments, because I felt I could not connect with him?" As she spoke, she realized all the pain she had been holding inside herself. It was only when she allowed herself to talk about her pain that she was truly vulnerable. At last, she was letting down her guard, and we accepted her into the program.

Vanessa really needed community to help her venture into her vulnerabilities and find inspiration again. She felt work was no longer motivating her. She confronted her inner struggles through the program and gained self-compassion as she understood that she did what she had to do to survive as a child. She realized she was no longer in danger, and there was no need for the emotional armor she wore. She learned the importance of self-love. She was grateful for the skills of self-preservation she had learned as a child, and she thanked the little girl inside for protecting her.

Finally, Vanessa moved herself from a mindset of self-preservation. She needed to evolve from a child to an adult with gratitude. She reminded herself that as an adult she was now safe—no one could ever hurt her the way she had been hurt as a child, and she no longer had to carry her armor.

As Vanessa's evolution took place, I witnessed her develop a gracious, peaceful, and loving energy that she began to exude to others, especially those she met at work. The transformation was one of the most remarkable acts of transformation I have ever witnessed in my life. I still get sensitive and cry at times when I think of the beauty of Vanessa's human evolution.

Vanessa decided to stay at the organization she was with, but reframed her leadership approach by committing herself to do as much as she could to build a sense of belonging. Given her parameters at the organization, she has become a remarkably thriving leader, and her relationships at work are now built on true authenticity. She also became an advisor in our Institute in order to help other women as they move forward on their own journey. She continues to share her story, holding space for other women leaders to share their crucibles and rise beyond their own self-limitations.

Vanessa's family is extremely grateful for our leadership program and the impact it had on her. Her son shared with her this beautiful message: "Thank you for being present now, Mommy. Before the program, although you were with me, I never truly felt you were fully present. Your mind was always on work. I have fun with you now. It's different now."

Her husband attributes the work she did in the program with enhancing their marriage. He supports her as she continues her quest in supporting other women to become better humans and better leaders.

Vanessa's story is the story of thousands of women who go through our program. I witness again and again how these women remove their self-limitations by fully embracing their inner struggles and replacing those barriers with peace, love, self-compassion, and healthy boundaries. The result is so much self-awareness, getting clear on their values, and removing inhibitions. This helps them leave space for growth and evolution and allows them to become the best human beings possible. They cease judging others, realize everyone has baggage, and come to understand that they can be kind while still holding others accountable. They acknowledge they can be hard on the problem while not being hard on the person.

When I saw the continuous transformations of my students into better humans and better leaders, I was inspired to conduct an interview. Gathering over a hundred of my clients, graduates, and current students—as well as their bosses, colleagues, husbands, wives, children, mothers, and siblings, friends—I asked:

- Do you believe she is a better person now?
- Do you believe after the introspective work that she did she is a better human being?

They all, without a moment's hesitation responded, "Yes!" Bosses, husbands, wives, children, you name it, they all answered overwhelmingly in the positive. Furthermore, I asked my students, clients, and graduates these questions:

- Do you feel you're a better human being?
- Do you now see and feel your value?

They all answered in a resounding "Yes!" Next, I asked their bosses and their colleagues:

- Do you feel they're a better leader?
- If so, give me an example.

First up is Tamaya. She was one of our students in our leadership program and an entrepreneur with her own legal employment firm. Law offices and legal firms go to her for assistance in hiring attorneys for their companies. She finds attorneys for them and places them in different companies. When she started her business, Tamaya worked hard and wanted to grow it.

One day, we were having lunch and she said, "You know, I really want to grow my company, but I'm struggling."

To this, I asked her how many people she is hiring. To my shock, she said she can't hire people because she can't trust people.

"What are you talking about?" I asked, perplexed.

Tamaya sighed. "I need to just do this on my own because employees can't be trusted."

Shocked, I asked, "Who told you employees can't be trusted? I have employees, and they're amazing."

Tamaya averted her gaze. "My mother always taught me that you just can't trust people. People can't be trusted, so you just need to stick to family."

"With all due respect to your mother," I said, "you're 42 years old. You're still listening to your mom? You are an adult woman who can now make decisions on your own. You don't have to believe what you were taught as a child. You can choose to believe something different."

Tamaya was silent, then replied, "Yes, you're right. I could. I never really thought about it like that."

"Do you realize," I continued, "that the belief you had as a child has now gotten in the way of you expanding your business and leaving a legacy for your children?"

"Oh, my gosh." Tamaya's eyes widened. "You're right. I never thought of it that way.

It blew Tamaya away to realize that her lack of trust in people was negatively impacting her life and career. So, what would she do? With my help, she was able to identify the root of her self-limiting beliefs—especially her lack of trust—and overcome it through introspection and connecting with other women who have similar experiences. Today she has fifteen employees whom she trusts very much. The day we had lunch, she was the sole employee with a $900K annual revenue. Now, her company is worth millions. Tamaya continues to go out of her way to examine other limiting beliefs that may be inhibiting her growth. She isn't only growing for her company but for her beautiful marriage as well.

Her husband shared this in his speech during her graduation: "I've seen my wife, through this program, stand up straighter and walk taller. In this very short period of time, I've witnessed her transform from successful career woman to a decisive, focused leader who is clearly taking it to the next level. Thank you so much for making my wife an even more amazing wife, a better human being, and a better mother."

Tamaya was able to identify her limiting beliefs and realize that they were getting her into destructive patterns and inhibiting her business. Once she relinquished her mistrust of others, her business flourished, as did all the other areas of her life. Tamaya became a better human and also a better leader.

This is true of the many women who come into our program. Their stories are unique, but their transformations into better humans and better leaders are very similar and equally powerful.

The first year of the leadership institute, one of our students was having difficulty making a transformational breakthrough. She called me, clearly upset, and said, "I don't understand why I am not having a breakthrough. All the other women are saying that they're experiencing transformations. But I'm not."

As we got into the conversation further, I reviewed her coursework and realized she was not being introspective. She was not doing any deep self-examination. She was being diplomatic in her responses to all the questions. And so, I asked her, "Why don't you want to be honest with yourself?"

Confused, she insisted, "I am being honest with myself."

I had to be firm. "No, you're not. You're not speaking the truth. You're just being very diplomatic."

"My father taught me my entire life to be diplomatic," she replied, "and it has worked for me. There's no need to change it now."

"I understand," I said, doing my best to validate her. "But I'd like to share something with you. You will never go through a transformation being diplomatic. The only way you're going to go through a transformation is through deep introspection and self-examination. Unless you choose to do that, you will not be going through any type of transformation. However, a day may come when you will encounter an obstacle, and you will come face-to-face with the depths of your soul. You will have no other choice but to do a deep dive into yourself in order to move forward in a holistic,

You will never go through a transformation being diplomatic. The only way you're going to go through a transformation is through deep introspection and self-examination.

emotionally healthy way as a leader and human being. The day it happens, come back to me and I will help and work with you. Until then, there's nothing I can do for you." The reality for some individuals who do not want to do deep self-reflection is that there is nothing we can do for them.

In 2019, I gave a speech at our Leadership Institute's annual graduation. I would like to share it with you.

The most precious of all gems is the diamond. This global symbol of love, power, and perfection is created under immense pressure and extreme temperatures. The diamond is also the hardest of all known natural substances. In fact, it's only possible to cut a diamond into a brilliant multifaceted work of art by using another diamond.

Ladies and gentlemen, this is the essence of our leadership program. We utilize the life experiences and qualities a woman already possesses to transform her into a diamond. This remarkable leadership program is a journey like no other. It is a holistic transformation of mind, heart, and soul, and a journey that begins with a deep dive into the individual's spiritual and personal history. These life experiences are called our crucibles. All the positive accomplishments, all the negative trials and tribulations, all the successes and failures—each is revealed and measured for its effect on each woman's growth and achievement.

We know positive experiences reinforce dreams and goals, but real change and true strength is often found in the challenges and hardships we've experienced on the job. We don't always know the personal disappointments, the dark residue of emotional, physical, or sexual abuse, or the obstacles that stand between us and true happiness. But like a diamond in the making, each participant is able to find the inner fortitude to face those crucibles head-on and use them to make themselves stronger.

The word diamond comes from the Greek term meaning unconquerable. That's exactly what the graduates of this program are. Unconquerable. They are ready to conquer every challenge that comes before them with grace and love. The program creates an awareness of their greatness, and once a woman knows and embraces who she is, there is no turning back. She can't unknow it. The glass ceiling is shattered. Her dreams become grander. There's a revelation of a limitless future.

Our leadership program provides the environment, the structure, the safe space, if you will, for a woman to confront every past experience and embrace it and emerge as a stronger person and leader who has a sense of her true value and a laser focus on her goals. She becomes a leader committed to her life's mission. This shift in her mind allows her to embrace all of who she is and to step into the woman and the leader she is meant to be and reach a level of success she never imagined.

This major mind shift cannot be explained. It is a transformation that can only be experienced and witnessed. What is so remarkable about these women is that this phenomenal shift leads them to make a positive impact on the companies they lead, on the companies they own, on their families, and even on the very essence of their soul.

CONCLUSION

When life presents challenges to women, they react in a variety of ways. Some women tend to withdraw into themselves and become fearful and timid. While they may seem like agreeable team players on the outside, the truth is they are trapped in a cycle of pleasing others in order to prevent conflict, stress, and drama. This perceived graciousness is dangerous and self-destructive, and it holds them in bondage, preventing them from progressing in their lives and careers.

Other women build hard, nearly impenetrable shields around themselves to reduce the effects of disappointment, rejection, and harsh, often unfair treatment. These women become assertive in an attempt to strike before being struck, a combative defense mechanism that ensures they are in charge of making decisions concerning their lives and careers. Although assertive women are often respected for their tough, uncompromising demeanors, they can also be perceived as cold and selfish, causing those around them to become defensive.

In today's global society, leaders face a mountain of racial, cultural, emotional, and other difficult challenges. They cannot be perceived as weak or indecisive, or they will not be taken seriously, yet they also cannot become overly assertive and risk driving those around them into defensive shells. Both paths only serve to compound troublesome issues.

The solution has been mapped out in this book through the methodology of Graciously Assertive Leadership. This leadership style combines the best of both worlds to form a woman who is both gracious and bold. She knows how to take charge in a way that draws those around her into a unified team rather than a resistant force, leading to a safe, energetic, and productive environment. The Graciously Assertive Leader brings out the best in others because it requires her to make necessary changes in herself and become a better human.

The Graciously Assertive Leader brings out the best in others because it requires her to make necessary changes in herself and become a better human.

How does she do this? Well, she must adhere to the 8 Pillars of Graciously Assertive Leadership, all of which equip her with the tools to navigate difficult obstacles. These principles transform her from a fearful and timid woman—or a cold and aggressive one—into a leader who is approachable, in control, and sincerely respected. The Graciously Assertive woman gains the respect of those she leads and catches the attention of those under whom she serves, opening doors to opportunities and blazing trails of success.

The 8 Graciously Assertive Pillars are not only for those seeking leadership positions. Their transformative qualities also create better lives for all those who incorporate them. The Graciously Assertive woman experiences improved relationships, more respectful treatment, a more vibrant social presence, and so much more. The most treasured outcome of practicing these principles is freedom—freedom from the heavy shackles of the past and the unfair and judgmental attitudes of others. This freedom allows women to express who they truly are.

Graciously Assertive: How Becoming a Better Human Being Makes You a Better Leader gives everyone the necessary tools to excel in life. My hope is women from all racial and cultural backgrounds will use this book as a guide to transform themselves and assist others. Each precious woman who takes charge of her life and becomes a better human helps create a better world.

I want to thank all women who have exercised the courage to take my courses, have learned to embrace the Graciously Assertive Lifestyle, and have made strides in not only becoming better humans but improving those relationships within their sphere of influence. And I also want to thank all the future women who will see the light through the words in this book, the lessons from my conferences, or the testimonies of transformed lives. Here's to you all!

NOTES

1. Sylvia Ann Hewlett, "Likeability and Women's Leadership," *Harvard Business Review*, March 14, 2008, https://hbr.org/2008/03/likeability-and-womens-leaders.

2. R. J. Ely, H. Ibarra, and D. M. Kolb, "Taking Gender into Account: Theory and Design for Women's Leadership Development Programs," *Academy of Management Learning & Education* 10, no. 3 (2011), 474–93, https://doi.org/10.5465/amle.2010.0046.

3. Hewlett, "Likeability."

4. Janet B. Kellett, Ronald H. Humphrey, and Randall G. Sleeth, "Empathy and the Emergence of Task and Relations Leaders," *The Leadership Quarterly* 17, no. 2 (April 2006), 146–62, https://doi.org/10.1016/j.leaqua.2005.12.003.

5. Mikaela Beijbom, "Striving for Equity, Inclusion, and Safer Spaces at Work: A Review of the Literature," Live Work Well Research Centre, University of Guelph, November 2022, https://liveworkwell.ca/sites/default/files/pageuploads/Striving%20for%20Equity%2C%20Inclusion%2C%20and%20Safer%20Spaces%20at%20Work_Beijbom2022_AODA.pdf.

6. "What It Means to Be a Moral Leader," *Harvard Business Review*, September 22, 2023, https://hbr.org/2023/09/what-it-means-to-be-a-moral-leader.

7. Julian D. Ford et al., "Social, Cultural, and Other Diversity Issues in the Traumatic Stress Field," *Posttraumatic Stress Disorder* (2015), 503–46, doi:10.1016/B978-0-12-801288-8.00011-X.

8. Ibid.

9. "What It Means to Be a Moral Leader."

10. Aletheia Luna, "Spiritual Transformation: 9 Signs You're Evolving." LonerWolf.com, September 24, 2023, https://lonerwolf.com/spiritual-transformation/.

11. Ibid.

12. Donald Sull and Charles Sull, "The Toxic Culture Gap Shows Companies Are Failing Women," *MIT Sloan Management Review* 64, no. 3 (2023), 1–9, https://sloanreview.mit.edu/article/the-toxic-culture-gap-shows-companies-are-failing-women/.

13. Ibid.

14. *Psychology Today* staff, https://www.psychologytoday.com/us/basics/imposter-syndrome.

15. 2019 Dr. Yasmin Davidds Leadership Institute.

16. Ibid.

17. Ibid.

18. Ibid.

19. Trang Doan and Mai Iskandar-Datta, "Does Gender in the C-Suite Really Matter?," *Journal of Accounting, Auditing & Finance* 36, no. 1 (2021), 81–107, https://doi.org/10.1177/0148558X18793267.

20. 2019 Dr. Yasmin Davidds Leadership Institute.

21. Ibid.

22. Lydia Blanco, "Sheryl Sandberg: Black Women Have Been Leaning In for a Long Time Because There Was No Choice," *Black Enterprise*, December 17, 2019, https://www.blackenterprise.com/sheryl-sandberg-black-women-have-been-leaning-in-for-a-long-time-because-there-was-no-choice/.

23. 2019 Dr. Yasmin Davidds Leadership Institute.

24. Alanna Vagianos, "Michelle Obama on Leaning In: 'That S**t Doesn't Work All the Time,'" HuffPost, December 3, 2018, https://www.huffpost.com/entry/michelle-obama-lean-in_n_5c05319ee4b04fb2116a2ad9.

25. Camille Dundas, "Why Black Women Are Still Cringing at the Lean In Strategy," People of Color in Tech, January 1, 2020, https://peopleofcolorintech.com/articles/why-black-women-are-still-cringing-at-the-lean-in-strategy/.

26. Daphna Motro et al., "The 'Angry Black Woman' Stereotype at Work," *Harvard Business Review*, January 31, 2022, https://hbr.org/2022/01/the-angry-black-woman-stereotype-at-work.

27. "Inclusion in the Workplace," National University blog, accessed February 29, 2024, https://www.nu.edu/blog/inclusion-in-the-workplace/.

28. "Bridging Perspectives, Unlocking Potential," Intercultural Development Inventory, accessed February 29, 2024, https://www.idiinventory.com/.

29. Martyn Barrett (ed.), *Interculturalism and Multiculturalism: Similarities and Differences*, Council of Europe, 2013.

30. "Implicit Bias," American Psychological Association, accessed February 29, 2024, https://www.apa.org/topics/implicit-bias.

31. Erika Gutierrez et al., "Socialization and Culture," *Race and Ethnic Relations in the U.S.: An Intersectional Approach*, accessed February 29, 2024, https://socialsci.libretexts.org/Bookshelves/Social_Justice_Studies/Race_and_Ethnic_Relations_in_the_U.S.%3A_An_Intersectional_Approach/04%3A_Prejudice_Discrimination_and_Racism/4.01%3A_Socialization_and_Culture.

32. "Introduction to Power, Privilege, and Social Justice," Dartmouth University, accessed February 29, 2024, https://students.dartmouth.edu/opal/education/introduction-power-privilege-and-social-justice.

33. "Goodman Group Sustainability Report 2022," Goodman, accessed February 29, 2024, https://2022sustainabilityreport.goodman.com/people-and-culture/.

34. Agatha Agbanobi and T. Viva Asmelash, "Creating Psychological Safety for Black Women at Your Company," *Harvard Business Review*, May 22, 2023, https://hbr.org/2023/05/creating-psychological-safety-for-black-women-at-your-company.

35. "What Is Psychological Safety?," McKinsey & Company, July 17, 2023, https://www.mckinsey.com/featured-insights/mckinsey-explainers/what-is-psychological-safety.

36. Tanya Golash-Boza, "What Is Intersectionality?," August 30, 2019, https://www.youtube.com/watch?v=X-xZKHhdMEc.

37. "Sense of Belonging," Cornell, accessed February 29, 2024, https://diversity.cornell.edu/belonging/sense-belonging#:~:text=Belonging%20is%20the%20feeling%20of,their%20authentic%20self%20to%20work.

38. "Culturally Responsive Teaching Strategies: Importance, Benefits & Tips," American University, December 5, 2019, https://soeonline.american.edu/blog/culturally-responsive-teaching/.

39. "Self-Authorship Theory," University of Tennessee, accessed February 29, 2024, https://uthsc.edu/tlc/self-authorship.php#:~:text=Theory%20of%20Self%2DAuthorship&text=From%20Kegan's%20(1994)%20work%2C,269).

40. Angela Locks, "Summary of Yosso's Cultural Wealth Model," accessed February 29, 2024, https://studentaffairs.ucmerced.edu/sites/studentaffairs.ucmerced.edu/files/documents/yosso_summary_.pdf.

41. Saul Mcleod PhD, "Social Identity Theory in Psychology (Tajfel & Turner, 1979)," Simply Psychology, October 5, 2023, https://www.simplypsychology.org/social-identity-theory.html.

42. "Cultural Awareness," *Collins Dictionary*, accessed February 29, 2024, https://www.collinsdictionary.com/dictionary/english/cultural-awareness.